"Membershift is a call to action for associations. In a world where associations get lost in the mechanics of operations, Membershift fearlessly challenges us to reorientate our associations to the one thing that sets us apart from other organisations – our members. With a 'membership is everything' approach at its core, Sarah provides us with a blueprint for association leaders at all levels to re-orientate, re-discover and reclaim the future of your association."

- Toni Brearley, CAE, Chief Executive Officer, Australasian Society of Association Executives

"Designed for all association leadership and teams, MemberShift is a collection of strategies, thought-provoking discussion prompts, ideas, and compelling calls-to-action to usher in radical change into our associations to be member-centric. While the future is uncertain and often intimidating, Sarah provides a clear path forward to start putting members first throughout your association—everything from high-level strategy, visioning, and strategic partnerships down to day-to-day operations!"

- Chris Beaman, CAE, Corporate Partnerships Officer

"MemberShift is timely, and the 'wrong path' concepts Sarah addresses in the book are spot on! All Board members should be required to read MemberShift when onboarding. Growing and retaining membership requires the right effort if an organization is to create a long-term approach to existence. It's going to be a work-in-progress and MemberShift is the best resource for the journey!"

- Deborah Curry, Chief Financial Officer

"MemberShift provides the crash course everyone in the association world should take! This book not only explains how member motivations have continuously transformed for the better part of 40 years, but provides tangible steps for creating systemic changes necessary for a sustainable, member-centric association that can thrive in the future. Read the book, do the homework, engage your team in these hard discussions, and start shifting your focus to the members!"

- Kaitlin Solomon, Membership Lifecycle Marketing

"This book delivers so many a-ha moments! Membership associations must change to meet the needs of new generations if they want to survive. MemberShift gives readers guidance on how to successfully change and how to engage young members as well as seasoned members, too. Love it!"

- Abby Perdue, Membership Director

"Providing opportunities to think about the future in a concrete way while also allowing room for conversation about the unique aspects of each association, Sarah's book provides a framework for the future of membership and gives teams points for discussion. The membership model is changing, and Sarah provides tangible solutions to meet the needs of today's associations. I hope all associations take advantage of the insights and use the knowledge to move their organizations forward!"

- Jeanette Gass, Senior Program Manager of Global Engagement

"When working with boards of directors I frequently remind them that their sole asset is the membership. In *MemberShift* Sarah states: 'Without membership, skills aren't advanced, policies aren't developed, and industries aren't protected. Membership brings people together to collectively innovate, create, and mobilize.' I really enjoyed the interactive aspect of this book and believe it will be a great tool to guide boards of directors in their strategic work to define their 'why'."

- Sharon Kneebone, IOM, FASAE, CAE

MEMBER*SHIFT*

WHY MEMBERS LEAVE AND THE STRATEGIES PROVEN TO BRING THEM BACK

SARAH L. SLADEK

MEMBER*SHIFT*
Why Members Leave Associations and the Strategies Proven to Bring Them Back
by Sarah Sladek
1. BUS074030 | **BUSINESS & ECONOMICS** / Nonprofit Organizations
& Charities / Management & Leadership
2. BUS074000 | **BUSINESS & ECONOMICS** / Nonprofit Organizations
& Charities / General
3. BUS063000 | **BUSINESS & ECONOMICS** / Strategic Planning

ISBN: 979-8-88636-029-5 (paperback)
ISBN: 979-8-88636-031-8 (hardcover)
ISBN: 979-8-88636-030-1 (ebook)

Library of Congress Control Number: 2023910493

Cover design by Lewis Agrell

Printed in the United States of America

Authority Publishing
13389 Folsom Blvd #300-256
Folsom, CA 95630
800-877-1097
www.AuthorityPublishing.com

DEDICATION

To Patsy. My cheerleader, guide, advocate, and closest friend. My true north. My guardian angel. You will forever be a part of me. I miss you, Mom.

How to Use This Book

This book was designed to be an interactive learning experience. Here's how to use it:

- *Read and Review*
  Each chapter of the book tackles a concept in-depth. It's written like a playbook: Read about the strategy, then complete the charts and assessments and respond to the questions at the end of the chapter. Space is provided to write in this book and use it as your personal journal.

- *Team Up*
  It is strongly recommended readers organize a book club or discussion group within their associations to discuss and work through the concepts outlined in this book together. For example, if the team reads a chapter each month and intentionally sets aside time to discuss and work on the strategies together, by the end of the book, the team will have the beginnings of a member-centric plan developed and ready to immediately deploy.

- *Learn More*
  Visit the author's website to access additional book-related content and materials. www.sarahsladek.com

TABLE OF CONTENTS

PREFACE

Membership strategy. How much do we *really* know about it?

Membership is not a recognized subject of expertise.

There are no degrees in membership. The CAE (Certified Association Executive) designation delves into governance, executive leadership, and organizational management strategy—but not membership. A nonprofit management degree doesn't cover membership either.

From plumbers to astrophysicists, there are few occupations that don't require prior experience or training specific to the job's responsibilities. But as it stands, there are no defined requirements, career paths, educational tracks, or training programs dedicated to membership.

In the United States alone, membership organizations employ 1.3 million people and generate $116 billion in revenue each year, and not a single person has been certifiably or definitively trained in the subject of membership.

Boards of directors lack training in the subject as well, yet they influence the key decisions of membership organizations, which rely on membership buy-in, sustainability, and growth.

Imagine walking into a financial institution and discovering no one who worked there had financial training, or walking into a healthcare organization and realizing no one had medical training. Would you not find it curious they were referring to themselves as an organization for which they had no expertise? And yet, this is a universally accepted standard for membership associations.

Do you realize what this means?

It means that all this time, the strategies essential to membership engagement and growth—including knowledge of the changing psychological, sociological, marketing, and economic drivers that impact membership growth—have remained largely unknown, overlooked, guessed, or left to chance.

Like the continent of Antarctica, membership has remained largely unexplored.

Perhaps we believed membership was a natural state of being, and the subject didn't warrant further research, training, or expertise. After all, membership is the state of belonging within a group of people. This means we're all members of something—families, communities, faith-based organizations, political parties, schools, teams, causes, and clubs—so perhaps there was just an assumption we all innately know and understand the concept of membership strategy.

Plus, the concept of membership organizations emerged in the 1600s and survived wars, disease, and recession. Why would now be any different? Perhaps we took comfort in knowing associations and membership have long been tenets of society and an integral part of who we are as individuals and communities. Perhaps we thought membership would forever be the same, and that would never change.

But it did.

During these past few decades, how we build community and achieve a state of belonging has changed. We're living in an era of disruption marked by the unprecedented speed of change, including advancements in technology, economic fluctuations, globalization, and demographic shifts. Everything about the way we live, work, and do business has evolved in a relatively short period. As a result, approaches to community-building and membership strategy evolved.

Or at least, they should have.

In 2011, I wrote *The End of Membership As We Know It: Building the Fortune-Flipping, Must-Have Association of the Next Century,* which explored the many social disruptions influencing changes in our tried-and-true membership models.

I've since realized it isn't just the models that need to change. It's thinking about community-building in entirely new ways. It's less about the what or how of membership and more about the who and why. The latter part is what's missing. Without it, associations can launch many new programs or initiatives or tinker with everything from dues to messaging, but the impact will be insignificant.

I've made three key discoveries since writing *The End of Membership*. All three will be examined in this book:

- What drives and influences membership growth remains unexamined and unknown.
- Membership isn't a strategic or operational priority for most associations.
- Despite being organized as communities of belonging, associations have struggled to be inclusive of young people.

Therefore, I concluded a new approach to membership is needed—a member-centric approach and shift to prioritize the members.

At first glance, this viewpoint might not make any sense. You may ask yourself, "But isn't our organization already member-centric? Isn't membership the mission, vision, and raison d'être of all associations?"

Not likely.

Maybe you haven't realized it. Maybe the phenomenon hasn't been identified or labeled. But in nearly every association I've studied, closer analysis reveals that membership is not the priority.

This didn't just happen.

In 2001, I resigned from my role at a membership association and started researching membership engagement. At the time, associations were experiencing their first encounters with noticeable membership decline. It was a relentless trend that would continue to plague associations, which eventually spurred my interest in writing *The End of Membership*.

What was happening then is still happening now.

Generation X (1965–1981) was entering the workforce, and they became the first generation known for questioning the value of a membership. They didn't join associations en masse like preceding generations. When this happened, rather than seeking to understand why, the initial reaction was one of criticism. Gen X became labeled as non-joiners, slackers, and the what's-in-it-for-me generation.

As an Xer myself, I didn't appreciate the stereotypes. I'd spent my youth volunteering for associations, as well as observing my parents in their volunteer leadership roles for many membership organizations. I knew my generation *could* be joiners, but they didn't want to be because they didn't feel like they belonged. Raised during a time of increased social change, Xers were seeking new and different membership experiences. They wanted to align with communities who understood them and were open to change—two concepts membership organizations were struggling to comprehend.

Regrettably, the pattern has continued to repeat itself. Why?

Simply put, it's because associations excel at the what and how parts of membership. They have mastered what they do and how they do it, and all the related processes, practices, and traditions. Where they struggle is the who and why.

What I've learned is, when an organization is so intently focused on the what and how, there's little room for innovation or empathy, and purpose and people inevitably get pushed to the side. Over time, this has created gaps, disengagement, and decline as associations have strayed further and further away from their missions and members.

For the past few centuries, membership was a reliable continuity; associations were run a certain way, people joined and actively participated, and traditions were formed and passed down from generation to generation. Focusing on the what and how was beneficial to the building of membership communities. But for the past few decades, membership has been utterly and completely disrupted by the who and why, which means the what and how has also been disrupted.

Is there any hope for the future of membership?

Yes! But only if associations can remember why their organizations were started in the first place and make a committed effort to create communities of belonging for members representing all ages and career stages. Until now, much about membership has been a mystery, unexplored and unexamined. That ends now. We're done with winging it and just hoping for the best.

I have spent the past two decades researching shifts and trends within our society and their impacts on belonging, community-building, and membership. Realizing there wasn't a go-to guide or training on the topic, I delved into understanding membership for myself. I've earned my own MBA in membership, and I'm writing this book in the hope that it will help save associations from further disengagement and decline.

And so, dear reader, this book is the training you never received to help you succeed in a role for which you were likely never prepared. May it help you engage members, grow membership, and build a vibrant membership community.

If you forget everything you read in this book, I hope you will remember this: Your association's future success relies solely on its ability to be member-centric. Nothing else matters.

CHAPTER 1

THE END OF MEMBERSHIP

Associations must evolve, and they must do so at the same pace as the rest of society. If they can't keep up, don't define the future, and ignore the changing demographics, associations risk becoming obsolete. It's already happening, and it's about to accelerate.

– Sarah Sladek, *The End of Membership As We Know It* (2011)

W hy did you choose membership?

When you were young, you likely weren't dreaming about growing up and going to work for an association. As you grew, chances are you weren't reading about membership careers in books or learning about them at job fairs or anywhere else.

And you didn't earn a degree in membership—a post-secondary educational track for membership doesn't exist. Even association management is a rare find in terms of education tracks.

This means you walked into a role with little prior knowledge or training, either discovering the opportunity by chance or because someone told you about it and invited you to consider it.

Of all the opportunities available, why did you agree to do something you weren't planning to do, prepared to do, or trained to do?

Why membership? This is a question rarely asked, and when it is, the most common responses typically fall into one of two categories:

- "I fell into it." You learned on the job and were unaware of what an association did prior to taking on the role.
- "I don't do membership." This is usually followed up with a statement like, "I work for an association, but not in the membership department" or, "I sit on the board, but we don't make decisions about membership."

Neither response supports the notion membership organizations are on the right path. Associations engage millions of employees and volunteers, but with limited membership training and resources available, they are forced to rely on historic models or innovate under pressure, and both yield less than favorable results.

It is curious, isn't it? The decision to work for or volunteer with a membership organization is often described as something akin to the book *Alice in Wonderland*. Somehow, you fell through a rabbit hole, ending up in a fantasy world you never knew existed. And just like Alice, an identity crisis ensues, and you wonder how you got there because membership isn't your area of expertise. In fact, you don't really know much about membership at all.

Clearly, associations weren't intended to be wonderlands that people fall into and try to figure out. But membership has changed since its boom days, requiring associations to also change and re-examine how they inform, inspire, and otherwise align people to their missions and the critical work they do.

I believe systemic change needs to happen, but to design the future is to understand the past. So, let's go back to the end—the end of membership as we know it.

THE BEGINNING OF THE END

The 1940s launched an era of growth for membership organizations. It was a post-war era—World War II ended, and communities were inspired to rebuild and reconnect in a time of peace. The Baby Boomer generation (1946–1964) was born into this social structure. They became the largest generation in history, and they were told they represented hope, rebuilding, and the start of a peaceful future.

In the aftermath of war, a strong desire to feel secure, stable, and connected emerged. People wanted to be a part of something positive and meaningful and in community with others. As a result, membership organizations boomed.

In fact, membership morphed into a social expectation. Membership was a way to showcase your commitment to improve and build community. Literally referred to as the "right thing to do," people enthusiastically joined many membership groups, from bowling leagues to Boy Scouts, golf clubs to service clubs, YMCAs, and professional and trade associations.

For three decades, associations prospered. Then, suddenly and seemingly without warning, the growth came to a screeching halt in the 1990s. This changed everything as associations everywhere were hit with the realization that young people weren't joining associations in the same numbers as previous generations.

After decades of prosperity, it seemed unlikely there was anything wrong with the membership model itself. Anxious, confused, and looking for a reason, a rumor took root that something was different about "kids these days." In fact, the generation coming of age—Generation X (1965–1981)—became the first generation to be publicly criticized for their lack of organizational involvement. They became renowned in media, workplaces, and membership organizations as the non-joiner, slacker, what's-in-it-for-me generation. There's no doubt about it: Gen X ushered in a shift that would forever change society's views of membership and social contracts with membership organizations.

Initially, this spurred widespread disbelief and denial. I started working for a membership association in the late 1990s. Even though I fell into the age category the organization was desperately trying to reach, my insights were largely ignored. Perplexed by the severity and magnitude of the situation, the desperation among leaders to create a new reality became palpable. Affirmations like these were happening daily:

> This is temporary! It's nothing to worry about. Eventually, membership will bounce back. We just need to give it time. Young people will grow up and realize they need to join. This is just a phase. They are just being immature. We'll get through this. Soon, everything will go back to normal. Just you wait and see.

Research continued to prove a shift had occurred, and the call for change kept coming. Still, the struggle to accept and adapt to this new normal would end up plaguing associations for the next several years. Consider the following timeline:

- 1994: Membership decline makes national headlines, cited as a concerning trend reported by organizations of various types and sizes.
- 2000: Robert Putnam's book, *Bowling Alone: The Collapse and Revival of American Community*, featured data showcasing an aggregate decline in membership of traditional civic organizations.
- 2004: Numerous media reports spanning the globe covered the story of declining membership.
- 2005: A *Journal of Association Leadership* article explored the "disappearance of the traditional association member base," classified as a white, 50-to-60-year-old homeowner, upper

educated, urban based, married, with a higher-level job. The article urged associations to prepare for rapidly approaching, significant demographic shifts.

- 2006: The *Washington Post* reported on declining membership engagement among Generation X. The article cited research projecting Xers would be interested in joining associations when they hit their peak earning years, but only if associations provided tangible services and real evidence that joining was good for their careers.
- 2010: National Public Radio reported on the robust history of trade associations, citing the fact that during the past 10 years, many had struggled to survive.
- 2011: American Sociological Association research, taking place between 1994 and 2011, revealed active membership in civic groups, fraternal organizations, and other local associations had declined 6 percent. Generational differences were cited as one of the contributing factors.
- 2012: According to U.S. Chamber of Commerce Foundation research, 62 percent of professional associations were experiencing flat or declining membership. Associations with 5,000 or more members reported the greatest challenge was engaging the membership of younger generations.
- 2014: Pew Research's *Millennials in Adulthood* study discovered the Millennial generation (born 1982–1995) has fewer attachments to traditional institutions, including membership organizations.
- 2019: According to the *Membership Growth Report*, 68 percent of membership organizations surveyed reported flat or declining membership.
- 2021: Findings for the *Membership Marketing Benchmarking Report* revealed nearly half (47 percent) of associations surveyed experienced membership decline. In addition, 45 per-

cent reported declines in member renewals—up significantly from the previous year's 24 percent.

- 2022: According to the *Global Membership Health Study,* which surveyed association members and teams in 59 countries, 76 percent of associations globally are struggling to grow membership among young professionals ages 40 and under. In addition, survey results revealed gaps in member expectations and member value.

First established in the 1600s, associations have survived war, economic collapse, disease, and more. So why haven't associations been able to bounce back from the decline that first appeared in the 1990s? What makes this era so different?

It's different for these two key reasons:

- The needs and interests of members changed.
- Membership stopped being the priority.

Let's explore each of these reasons in greater detail.

CHANGING NEEDS AND INTERESTS

Change happened. Well, members changed, but membership organizations did not. Members changed because changes in society influenced changes in human behavior and development.

Whoa. Sounds heavy.

It's not that hard to understand once you take a closer look. We're all experiencing these changes in behavior and development. You know they are there, but you may not notice or understand them. Consider this timeline, which briefly demonstrates why and how the needs of members changed.

- 1946–1964:

  The largest generation in history is born. It's a post-war era, so optimism for the future is prevalent, as is the desire to focus on family values and rebuild communities. As a result, the Baby Boomers were raised to value opportunity, stability, and community. They would grow up to become the wealthiest generation in history, moving into positions of power and influence and holding the workforce majority for 34 years. In 1964, the last of the Baby Boomers were born. It was a transitional year with the arrival of an entirely new music genre—rock 'n roll—and Beatlemania. Plus, Congress passed the Civil Rights Act prohibiting discrimination based on race, color, religion, sex, or national origin.

- 1965–1981:

  Change sped up, and Generation X was accurately named X to resemble being born at the crossroads of cultural and social change. Society was awakened to new voices and ideals influenced by the generation coming of age alongside the Civil Rights and Women's Rights Movements, the Vietnam War, skyrocketing divorce rates, the impeachment of President Nixon, Live Aid, and the launch of cable television. Gen X was the first generation to be raised valuing customization, globalization, and work-life balance.

- 1982–1995:

  The personal home computer was introduced in 1982, appropriately signifying the start of a new generation—one that would never know life without technology. Generation Y, also known as Millennials, would outnumber the Boomers to become the largest generation globally. They hold the titles of being the most-studied, most-debt-ridden, most-protected, most-supervised, and most-provided-for generation in history. In addition to coming of age alongside technology and the Great Recession, this generation's development was influenced by terrorism, school shootings, increased pressure to achieve in college and career, student debt, and helicopter parenting.

- 1996–2009:
  Generation Z becomes the first generation raised using mobile technology and social media. Research proves their brains have developed differently, largely due to the influx of information via technology. They are the most diverse generation in history, and the first to be raised with a minority American president, anti-bullying campaigns, and the Marriage Equality Act. Equality is the rule, not the exception. Zs create and consume more content than any other generation, have reported higher levels of anxiety and depression, and have been more involved in activism. Other influences key to their brain and social development include political conflict, gun violence, climate change, the wave of start-ups, protests, a global pandemic, and the George Floyd incident.

Membership decline was first cited as a trend in the 1990s. That's not a coincidence. By this time, most Gen Xers had transitioned into the workforce. They were seeking something different from what associations provided, but accepting change took time and responding to change proved equally difficult. Associations have struggled to re-engage members ever since.

To be crystal clear, belonging didn't change. Membership is not dead. And what happened isn't the result of a character flaw that somehow popped into the DNA of the generations born since the mid-1960s.

Belonging is something we all want and need. It's human nature to want to be included and feel you are part of a community and making a connection and a difference. Membership still matters; it's the needs and interests of members that have changed.

The word "change" sounds simplistic. Rarely do we examine the brevity of this change under harsher light. The fact is that change has been a struggle because the change that's happening isn't something we've learned to respond to or even understand. Everything about the way we live, work, and do business has changed or is in the process of changing, and this amount of change is unprecedented. At no other time in history has life-altering, brain-development change happened this often.

Let that sink in for a moment.

We're not talking about something turnkey or simple to master. This is not "change your mind to pick chocolate ice cream instead of vanilla" kind of change. It's not even the "change your address" or "change your job" kind of change. This is different. This isn't just about you. It's about everyone experiencing something new, creating a monumental shift in how we all decide and communicate and what we value and expect.

This is social change.

And while every generation observes and experiences change, the youngest generations are affected by the change developmentally. As children and adolescents, both brain development and social development are happening, and both are influenced by socializing agents. What we experience at home and via the world is key to development, which is why generations exist.

On a macro level, people raised during the same era are shaped by many of the same social influences and end up forming similar responses to those influences. On a macro level, society observes the end of one era and the beginning of another.

It took more than a decade to be considered a trend, but the real start of the membership declines likely began in 1982. When technology went mainstream and computers entered our homes, the Industrial

Era officially ended. Yes, the Industrial Era was founded in the 1700s. And yes, many associations are still holding on to the Industrial Era.

Think about it. In the Industrial Era, linear thinking and processes were prominent. Organizations relied on hierarchies, processes, rules, and traditions. (Still have some of those lying around? Of course, you do! Most organizations do.) However, the generations born since 1982 have little to no memory of Industrial Era methodologies and therefore no appreciation or understanding of processes, hierarchy, and doing things the way they've always been done. These generations were born into and only know a world powered by the trademarks of a world fueled by innovation, interconnectedness, globalization, and opportunity. Anything else will seem foreign and irrelevant to them.

What does this mean for your association? It means the generations born into the post-Industrial Era will struggle to comprehend why the bylaws can't be changed and decisions can't be made on the fly, why they can't have a seat at the decision-making table, and why it's always been done "that way." In this post-Industrial Era, human capital, innovation, and ideas have emerged as the most precious and coveted resources. As a result, this era has been referred to as the Talent Economy.

The needs and interests of members changed. When associations were slow to respond to this change, disengagement and decline followed.

Consider an alternate ending. Imagine associations remained singly focused on what members wanted and needed, quickly responding to meet those needs while remaining open to new ideas and change. The outcome would have been quite different. Associations would be prospering and growing exponentially, which isn't the case for most associations today.

As counterintuitive as it may sound, membership decline happened because membership organizations stopped paying attention to the members.

Membership stopped being the priority.

MEMBERSHIP ISN'T THE PRIORITY

When the membership slide was first cited as a trend in the mid-1990s, panic set in, and associations clutched their proverbial pocketbooks. This decision ended up backfiring, shifting attention away from community-building and severely diluting the member value proposition.

A drop-off in membership meant associations experienced a drop-off in dues, so many associations diversified their revenue streams. In theory, this was a good idea and a healthy business practice, but over time, the focus shifted from people to profitability. Associations abandoned their member-centric missions, focusing instead on producing numerous or large-scale events and public services. The idea was to cast a wider net, be accessible to as many people as possible, and the revenues and membership would surely follow.

Except they didn't.

This is because membership organizations started acting like businesses that also happened to offer a membership option. Membership was downgraded, becoming the optional side order as in, "Would you like a side of bacon with your eggs?"

Is membership the bacon or the eggs at your association? Are you making choices that will put your association on the path to growth and success—or sustained decline?

Here's a list of seven signs that may indicate the association is on the wrong path:

Supported by event revenue · Focused on non-members · Not represented in leadership · Focused on recruiting · Board not reflective of membership · Tries to be everything to everyone · Delayed outreach to young people

Let's explore each of these in greater detail.

- *The association is largely supported by event revenue.*

  During the global pandemic, associations were reporting crip-pling revenue losses—as much as 60 to 70 percent—due to the cancellation of their annual conferences. This raises the question of purpose and focus. It's rare to encounter associa-tion planning conferences that are exclusive to members only, but it's common to find associations dedicating a considerable amount of staff time to event planning or relying almost exclu-sively on the revenues generated by events. Where's the mem-ber value in these non-member offerings? If you're not sure, then be careful. It's possible your association has lost sight of its mission and morphed into an event planning company.

- *The association focuses on non-member participation.*

  As mentioned above, there's a misguided belief that member-ship will grow when associations open the doors to give access and provide value to the masses. When non-members are given equal access for a slightly higher cost, or the same cost, the value of membership is lost. Are there as many non-members as members attending events and utilizing services? Is the as-sociation actively launching and supporting community and industry-wide initiatives? If so, then membership decline is in-evitable. When members don't have a clear advantage, associa-tions think and act like a nonprofit providing a public service.

- *The association doesn't focus on membership at the leader-ship level.*

  As membership engagement efforts grew in complexity, there wasn't a move to invest in membership research, training, and outreach. Rather, associations largely shifted focus, investing in events, corporate sponsors, and other non-dues revenue streams. They even turned to technology companies to solve the membership problem, believing online communities, apps, and platforms were the answer. Whether ignored or delegated, membership stopped being the central focus. It makes little sense that the membership part of a membership organization would be MIA at the executive level. Membership should be an executive priority and an integral part of operations. Every association should regularly provide membership training to board members, chapter leaders, volunteers, and staff. And every association should have an MSO (membership strategy officer) or CMO (chief membership officer) as part of the executive team. If an association wants to engage members and grow membership, membership must be a strategic imperative.

- *The association focuses on recruiting.*
  The poet W. H. Auden wrote, "We would rather be ruined than changed." This applies to the associations that encounter decline and fail to ask why. Rather than look within to better understand why members are leaving, their first reaction is to recruit new members. This decision places them in a continual loop of growth and decline. This doesn't get to the root of what's causing the decline, and over time, this instability does considerably more harm, negatively affecting organizational culture, brand, and member experience. When decline happens, it's always better to double-down on understanding and fixing the problem. Innovate. Community-build. Invest in your culture. Membership isn't the priority when an association is fixated on recruiting new members rather than serving the members they already have.

- *The association tries to be everything to everyone.*
  I will never forget the time when I sat down with an association CEO who was lamenting his association's membership

decline. When I asked who the target market was, he gave me a list of 10 different audiences. "I just don't understand it," he said. "We appeal to so many people, but no one is joining." This is because when associations try to be everything to everyone, eventually, no one feels especially important, connected, or valued. It's always a better approach to go small and specialized than it is to go big and risk being inconsequential. Expanding to engage new audiences should be considered if, and only if, membership is healthy and growing, market saturation is nearing, and the association has the financial stability and bandwidth to expand reach strategically and intentionally over time. Membership isn't the priority when an association is focused on quantity rather than quality.

- *The association board isn't reflective of the membership community.*
  There was a time, not so long ago, when advanced education wasn't accessible to everyone, start-up businesses and innovation weren't the norm, and relationships and business transactions were limited by geography. We're living in a different era now. Leadership is no longer synonymous with job titles or limited by years of experience, nor is it exclusive to an age group, gender, or race. Membership isn't the priority if the membership community isn't reflected in your organization's leadership. The voices of the entire membership need to be represented in governance—not just a select few.

- *The association delayed efforts to engage young professionals.*
  There was ample warning. It was researched and widely published, as highlighted in the previous timeline. In fact, I wrote about the aging of associations and their struggle to engage young members in my first book, *The New Recruit* (2007).

I believed associations would evolve to be more inclusive of young people. I never imagined the state of aging would persist this long or be this significant. I'm shocked by the number of associations who just gave up on reaching a younger demographic, broadening their definitions of young professional to include people under age 50, ditching student programs, or otherwise making strides to further distance themselves from next-generation outreach. Membership is not the priority when associations fail to make room for everyone.

The needs of members changed, and associations lost their way. Membership was moved to the backseat so associations could focus on other projects, markets, and growth initiatives.

With most associations now experiencing flat or declining membership, it's imperative we bring belonging back.

MEMBERSHIP MATTERS

At the beginning of this chapter, I posed the question: Why membership? Why did you choose to take this job or volunteer for an association? Assuming you knew nothing about membership and may still be figuring it out, why did you fall through the rabbit hole and agree to do something you weren't prepared or trained to do?

I think it's because membership matters.

Membership influences change, advances skillsets, improves lives, and creates solutions. Membership helps, serves, and cares for many people. Without membership, skills aren't advanced, policies aren't developed, and industries aren't protected. Membership gives people a voice. Membership brings people together to collectively innovate, create, and mobilize. Membership gives people a place to belong and an opportunity to make a difference. There is no other segment of society that improves lives like membership organizations do.

Therefore, it's imperative we reverse the disengagement and decline.

I believe that's why you're here. To make membership matter. To serve people and build something that's sustainable, inclusive, and diverse. You're here to create a membership community that will be around for generations to come. This isn't someone else's responsibility. It's yours, and it's mine. It's ours. Together.

So, let's get started.

CHAPTER 1: DISCUSSION GUIDE

Reflect and respond. Write your answers in the book or download the playbook online and fill it out. Share and discuss with others in the association.

Why did you choose membership? What is it about working or volunteering in a membership organization that inspires you?

_____

_____

_____

_____

_____

_____

_____

What's a tipping point or transition you've observed since being a part of the association—a moment when it became apparent the needs and interests of members had changed?

_____

_____

_____

_____

_____

_____

_____

Which generation are you? Do you think your generation feels like they belong in the association? Why or why not?

_____

_____

_____

_____

_____

_____

After reading this chapter, where did you identify opportunities for improvement? What immediate changes are needed to place the association on a member-centric path?

_____

_____

_____

_____

_____

_____

*Homework:

During the next 30 days, ask as many people as possible under the age of 30 the following questions. Keep track of what people say. Ask your association colleagues to do the same. Then, at the end of 30 days, set aside time as a team to share your findings with one another.

- If our organization wanted to build a membership experience that was especially meaningful and valuable to you and your peers, what would that experience look like?
- Describe a time when you felt like you really belonged. What specifically did the organization do to make you feel that way?

CHAPTER 2

MEMBERSHIP MYTHS

Membership engagement is the emotional commitment the member has with an organization. Members who are highly engaged are devoted to the organization and its success.

"I know what membership is. Membership is just getting on the phone and telling people about us. That's all it takes to get people to join."

And if decline is happening?

"Then we just need to call more people!"

Regrettably, I've heard this conversation more than once. This is just one example of many that brings to light the fact that membership as a practice, much less a strategy, is largely unknown or misunderstood.

All too often, membership is treated like a consumer good. Something transactional. Like a box of cereal. The cereal isn't selling well, so the price is changed, the box is redesigned, and the cereal company reduces its overhead costs.

Withholding the name, I'll use the example of a notable association that made national news after experiencing significant membership decline. The organization was teetering on the verge of financial ruin.

Closer review of the details leading up to the organization's downfall revealed the association was using the cereal strategy.

For starters, the association revamped the dues (price change), redesigned the logo (package redesign), and laid off employees (overhead reduction). Despite all the radical changes, the association experienced little to no growth in membership.

As consumers, we can relate to the cereal scenario. It's easy to see why an association would use this same product-based approach to membership strategy. In the world of consumer goods, success is largely contingent on pricing, packaging, and promotion. This isn't the case with membership, though. Membership isn't transactional. It's relationship-, values-, cause-, and ROI-based.

You can't feel an emotional attachment to your favorite brand of cereal in the same way you do a membership community. You can't value it the same way, either. While you could value if a cereal's nutritional content supports your healthy lifestyle, that's not the same as valuing the community, professional development, and leadership opportunities a membership provides.

Products don't pull at our heartstrings in the same way membership does. When you join an association, you are making the decision to be a part of a community. In the process, you are making a statement to the world about who you are and what's important to you. Moreover, you are making a pact with the organization—showing your trust and ongoing commitment by making an investment. From the very start, emotions are involved. That same level of commitment doesn't exist with a product purchase.

Membership is powerful, which is why many business-to-consumer brands are trying to turn occasional buyers into loyal customers by positioning their products as memberships. Companies like Costco, Netflix, Hertz, and Delta were the trailblazers. Now, restaurants and retail stores alike are developing membership programs to try to forge a stronger connection to consumers.

Membership is not a one-time purchase or a quick fix or an it's-on-sale-so-I'll-buy-it decision. The decision to join and engage is steeped in emotion and reasoning, which is why attempts to tweak pricing, packaging, and promotion are largely ineffective at curbing decline.

An entirely different strategy is required when it comes to membership.

MEMBERSHIP 101

Just as there is a belief that membership growth is fueled by the sales tactics used by consumer brands, there are many other unknowns about what fuels vibrant membership experiences and cultures.

Remember: There is no formalized training in the field of membership. Critical mistakes have occurred for that simple fact. What I'm sharing here is the outcome of my years of experience working for and with associations and my work as both a researcher of membership trends and turn-around consultant to associations.

Consider this your crash course in membership, starting with some of the most common questions and areas of misunderstanding:

- What's our value proposition?
- How do I know if members are engaged?
- Why won't young professionals join?
- What incentives should we use to recruit new members?
- When is the right time to raise dues?
- When should we expand our membership market?
- Who on our team should be responsible for membership strategy?

WHAT'S OUR VALUE PROPOSITION?

A great value proposition is essential for any association hoping to clearly communicate to prospective members why it's different, better, and worth getting involved. It's a promise that your association can deliver value to members. It's the most persuasive reason people should notice your association and engage.

Your association's mission statement is an internal roadmap. It defines your association's purpose, why it exists, and whom it serves. It reminds leaders, staff, and members about what the organization does at its core.

In contrast, a value proposition is intended for sharing. It's how you acknowledge that you know what the members need and what the association does best to answer those needs. It supports your members' rationale for choosing to affiliate with your association, versus another association or no association at all, and supports the public's image of the association. It should be very straightforward and easy to understand.

A great value proposition will create a must-have membership offer by succinctly

- Solving a problem
- Being exclusive to members and difficult to find elsewhere
- Establishing trust; and
- Being credible.

Here's what many associations fail to realize. The value proposition is not something your association's leadership gets to decide. Rather, the members dictate the value proposition—or at least they should. Associations that are especially adept at having purposeful conversations with their members and prospective members, especially those who represent the next generation, are able to identify their most valuable offerings from the member's perspective.

Let's go back to the cereal. This is one area of consumer product purchasing where associations could learn a thing or two. If a product isn't selling, the company will usually conduct consumer research to find out why. Yet, it is rare to come across an association that regularly and consistently engages in membership research, member feedback sessions, focus groups, interviews, or town halls.

What if the association is spending time and resources on promoting concepts and products the members don't want? Then membership doesn't sell. Like a box of cereal that remains on the shelf, the product goes stale, becomes increasingly irrelevant, and struggles to bounce back.

How do I know if members are engaged?

There are many definitions of member engagement. Some people will tell you engaged members attend events. Others will tell you an engaged member is someone who volunteers for leadership roles.

As was covered in Chapter 1, changes in society influence changes in membership behaviors and expectations. It used to be membership was, in large part, a journey. Traveling to conferences. Going to meetings. Always going places to get access to something or someone. It was even a journey in terms of leadership. Board seats were reserved for people who paid their dues and earned a leadership role after a lengthy period.

Here and now, the journey approach to membership isn't effective. Rather, people are now looking for a membership to be an asset and a value to not only themselves but also others.

Many associations measure member engagement according to destination points on the membership journey, such as event attendance, web traffic, volunteerism, and so on. These are all outcomes of member engagement, but strictly defining engagement by how members utilize the membership is missing the bigger picture.

Membership engagement is the emotional commitment the member has with an organization. Members who are highly engaged are devoted to the organization and its success. This means member engagement is shaped by emotions, experiences, and relationships—not just in one sector or aspect of the association but across the *entire* organization.

An engaged member will be connected to the association in each of the following ways:

Mission: Members feel connected to the organization's mission, vision, brand, and goals. They understand the organization's strategy for success, and they are proud to be a member.	Work: Members feel the association's work is necessary and important. They are inspired and empowered to contribute to and further the association's efforts.	Culture: Members feel the organization is trustworthy and respectful. They believe the association cultivates a culture that is member-centric, future focused, inclusive, and fair.	Community: Members feel connected to one another. They believe the decision to join has made a positive difference in their lives as well as the lives of others.

As you review this table, you are likely thinking of members who are highly engaged, and those who are not engaged at all. As you can see, just showing up for a few events is not a definitive sign of member engagement.

Why is engagement important? Because engaged members are less likely to let their memberships lapse. If your association is experiencing a flat or declining membership, that's a strong indication members are feeling disengaged or on the verge of disengagement.

Members who are engaged are more likely to be enthusiastic, positive, and hold favorable opinions of the association. They are also more likely to have a sense of purpose and pride and enthusiastically (without prompting) encourage other people to join.

Have you ever encountered a toxic board member or committee member, someone who oozes negativity and frequently complains? This is why participation isn't an accurate indication of member engagement. Activity level isn't a measurement of how people are thinking or feeling toward the organization.

Understanding what member engagement is and how to get it is key to your association's success.

WHY WON'T YOUNG PROFESSIONALS JOIN?

"Young people today just aren't joiners." How many times have you heard someone make that statement? It's often used in frustration, accusing young people of being unreliable and unwilling to follow in another generation's footsteps.

It's easy to blame "kids these days," simplifying it to a generational stereotype or a pre-existing condition that repels young people from joining any membership organization. A blanket statement such as this is an easy way out. It's the answer that relieves organizations of any commitment or duty. It's as if leadership blew a collective sigh of relief, thinking to themselves, *Whew! Young people aren't joiners. Now we're off the hook and no longer held accountable to future generations. We'll just keep doing what we've always done, and all will be well.*

It's the easy answer, but it's not the right answer. And all is not well for these membership organizations.

The decision to join an organization is accompanied by more consideration and scrutiny than in years past. From employers to faith-based groups, service clubs, and membership associations, people no longer connect to organizations simply because it's what they are expected to do, told to do, or because it's what their parents did.

There's a myriad of reasons this happened, all tied to major social shifts, including but not limited to shifts in education, parenting, technology, demographics, politics, and economics. How people engage in and build community has changed and continues to change.

When I was conducting research for my book, *Knowing Y: Engage the Next Generation Now* (2014), I uncovered a key shift in the decision-making process younger generations use when deciding whether to join an association.

Here's a visual to explain the different processes:

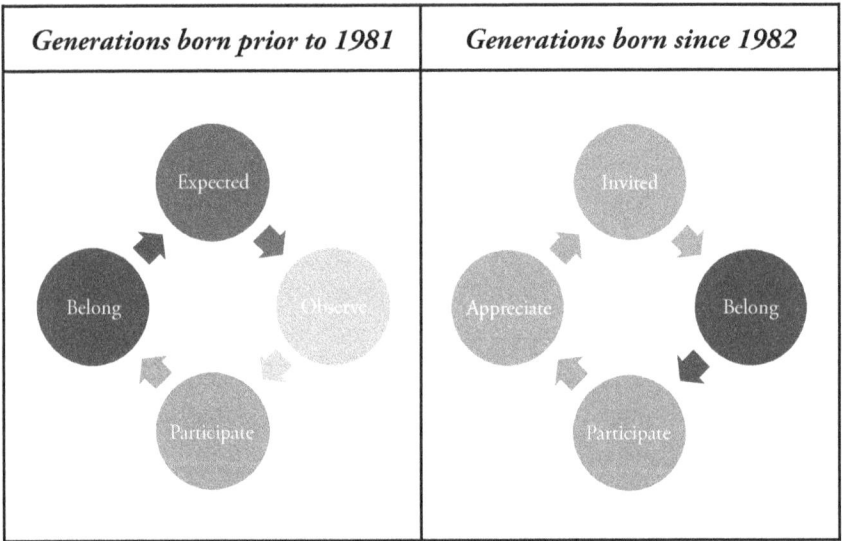

Generations born prior to 1981	*Generations born since 1982*
Expected / Observe / Participate / Belong	Invited / Belong / Participate / Appreciate

As you can see, for the generations born 1981 and earlier, the decision to join and become engaged in a membership organization doesn't look the same for the generations born since 1982.

Let's break it down.

	Phase 1	Phase 2	Phase 3	Phase 4
1981 and earlier	*Expected* Membership was a social expectation and the sign of good citizenship. Whether urged to follow in a parent's footsteps, heed a boss' advice, or do the research on their own to find an association to join, opting out wasn't a widely accepted option.	*Observe* Upon joining, there was much to learn. New members were expected to observe. Hierarchies, systems, and traditions were revered. Leadership was a privilege reserved for members with the most seniority. This is where the phrase "pay your dues" originates.	*Participate* As you became more established in your career or maintained your membership over a period, you were permitted to step into leadership and take a more visible, active role in the association.	*Belong* At this point, you felt a sense of belonging—or it was assumed you felt a sense of belonging—because you had been a member for many years, knew the process, and had forged a deeper connection between the members and the mission.

	Phase 1	**Phase 2**	**Phase 3**	**Phase 4**
1982 and after	*Invited* Membership is a choice. Research indicates these generations are less likely to join without a personal invitation from someone they know or admire. They rarely respond to social pressures or mass marketing efforts.	*Belong* Belonging must happen immediately. This means there are ample opportunities to get involved, the value is apparent, there's a greater call to action, and members feel welcomed into an organization that is positive, inclusive, and innovative.	*Participate* Deciding to join is deciding to get actively involved. These generations want to quickly move into volunteer and leadership roles and influence change. Participation is instantaneous, community driven, and action oriented.	*Appreciate* Members of all ages want to feel valued and important. They dislike it when their efforts are ignored or overlooked. Appreciation is important, especially since they chose to join and get involved (as opposed to feeling obligated).

The process we use to join organizations has shifted, but one thing remains the same: At the core of our being, all people want to belong. It's human nature. We all need and want to be in community with others, and we all want the communities we are living, working, and doing business in to be supportive of our needs and interests.

If young people aren't joining your association, there's a reason. And it's not a character flaw or personality problem or strange phenomenon. Rather than place blame and make assumptions, seek to understand. View the organization through their lens. Ask for their guidance and feedback. Then get to work on making some changes.

If young people aren't joining, there's a reason. And it's most likely because there is no place for them to belong.

WHAT INCENTIVES SHOULD WE USE TO RECRUIT NEW MEMBERS?

I've been asked this question many times, and my response has always been the same: Incentives don't work.

During the pandemic, associations focused on being accessible and supportive. When the going got tough, members appreciated access to free professional development courses and dues extensions. This was important and necessary. Members needed support, and associations provided it.

When the urgency of the crisis lessened with the arrival of vaccines, associations were seeking ways to maintain the momentum. This included the exploration of incentives.

Incentives can be meaningful, but don't make the mistake of thinking they will generate membership growth. Prospects will rarely make the jump to join solely to take advantage of a special offer or perk. These strategies are short sighted and ineffective at converting people to become engaged members.

Why? Because there are only two ways to influence a person's behavior: manipulation and inspiration. Manipulation works for a nanosecond, while inspiration leads to a more meaningful, long-lasting relationship.

Getting free stuff or discounts is awesome! But feeling invited and inspired to support a community or a cause, and feeling a sense of belonging is considerably more effective at generating growth. When members are engaged, they continue to renew, and they willingly invite others to join. Great membership experiences—within your current membership—is what drives growth.

Consider the story of the consultant tasked with increasing the profitability of an auto mechanic franchise. She visited the company's locations and interviewed employees and customers. A few months later, she sat down with the executives and said, "Want to increase sales? It's simple. Improve your waiting rooms."

The executives were upset. They were expecting to receive revolutionary marketing and customer-acquisition strategies guaranteed to drive increased profitability. But throughout the research, people repeatedly complained of the dark, dirty waiting rooms and unfriendly customer service. After one visit, most customers didn't return. Until this obstacle was cleared, revenue growth would prove difficult, if not impossible.

What's in your association's waiting room? What's the membership experience *really* like? If you want to drive membership growth, now is the time to take a closer look.

In the aftermath of the pandemic, organizations of all types and sizes will be vying for attention. Fueled by a life-is-short perspective, the market won't settle for experiences that feel negative, inadequate, or irrelevant.

Now, more than ever, people need to feel aligned to a mission, and they want to feel included in that mission. That's the best growth incentive by far.

WHEN IS THE RIGHT TIME TO RAISE DUES?

Dues have become a conundrum for associations, especially during the past two decades. Armed with technology and having observed large-scale economic shifts, people became more educated, careful consumers.

In fact, there have been three considerable shifts in consumerism that have changed how we buy and what we buy: the digital economy, the Great Recession, and a global pandemic. Today, members are likely to do research on an association and question the return on investment of a membership.

With so many Baby Boomers retiring, this has placed associations in a predicament of how best to recover from losses in dues revenue.

Perhaps it's best to first outline when *not* to increase dues. Dues bumps are a don't when

- Return on investment is limited
- The cost of membership is often cited as the reason people won't join or renew membership
- The association needs to increase short-term cash flow
- The association has a tradition of inflationary increases, raising prices according to a schedule
- Membership is flat or declining

In my work as a membership consultant, many associations struggling with decline have asked me to identify why. I've uncovered some red flags related to dues. Here's a snapshot of each.

- *Red flag 1: Limited ROI*

Membership will hit a roadblock when the cost-to-value ratio is askew. This means the cost for the membership exceeds the value, or the return on investment (ROI). All too often, non-members can access the same programs and services as members for a slightly higher fee via the association, and sometimes for free or a lower fee via another service provider.

It's not enough to say members receive the membership directory, the newsletter, event discounts, and representation in advocacy efforts. This describes a nice-to-have membership, not a must-have membership. The value is just too low. To retain and grow membership, the value of the membership must exceed the cost.

I urge associations to use the EIOU test when creating a menu of member benefits:

- E = Exclusive to members. Very difficult or very expensive for non-members to access it anywhere else. You must be a member.

- I = Included in the price of dues. Members don't have to pay an additional fee to access the benefit.
- O = Online. Accessible on-demand, online. Very tech forward to match the pace of the talent economy.
- U = Urgent. The benefit addresses an urgent and important need shared by the members.

When every other product and service the association provides is readily available to non-members, there's little to no advantage to being a member.

If you can't say with absolute confidence the value of a membership in your association exceeds the price of dues, then this is not the time to raise dues.

- *Red flag 2: Conference attendance is up, membership is down*

It's not a good sign if the association has become renowned for its conferences, but membership is flat or declining. When people are choosing to invest in the conference, but not the membership, it's either because the membership isn't considered valuable or because the cost of the conference is competing against the cost of membership. If the cost of a full conference registration is high enough, people may feel forced to choose where they invest their money—the conference or the membership.

It's important to remember that membership is a better long-term financial focus. Membership should generate more revenue for your association than events because membership—if done correctly—engages people year-round, and revenues will be consistent. Members are more likely to invest in the association on repeat, whereas non-members who are conference-goers will only invest in the annual conference and may not attend the conference every year.

Furthermore, if a large percentage of revenues rely on event attendance, this draws the association's attention and resources away from its actual mission, and the association begins to think and act like an event-planning company. The more the association distances itself from serving and prioritizing the needs of members, the more membership decline is likely to occur, challenging the organization's ability to engage members, grow membership, and generate sustained revenues.

If membership is flat or declining, do not raise dues.

- *Red flag 3: There isn't a strategic approach.*

Dues increases should never be approached as a quick-fix or fall under the category of tradition. By tradition I mean people are saying things like, "It's probably time to raise dues because we haven't in a while" or, "We have a tradition of raising dues every two years, and we need to uphold that tradition no matter what."

Changing the dues structure is a process that should take several months to effectively research, plan for, and communicate. Before any dues increase, do your due diligence by asking these questions:

- Do you have a compelling reason for raising dues?
- Did you get member feedback and buy-in prior to making the change?
- Did you take the time to communicate and explain the association's decision and how it will ultimately benefit the members?

Dues increases should always be accompanied by proof of the cost-to-value ratio, including communication on the latest investments and improvements the association has made to benefit members. Never put the association in a position where members are ill informed or put on the defensive, questioning the value and whether to renew.

If the association isn't well-prepared to make sure the members are well informed and part of the process, hold off on raising dues.

- *Red flag 4: People are unhappy.*

Besides assessing the ROI, membership trends, and doing your due diligence, it's equally important to assess how members are feeling. Remember: Member engagement relies on the emotional connection people have with the organization. If people are feeling skeptical, distrusting, or anxious, and the association moves forward with an ill-timed dues increase, the fall-out can be damaging.

It's a good time to rethink your dues strategy but not raise dues if any of the red flags mentioned above are present, or if people are feeling uncertain or unhappy.

Don't raise dues if:

- One of the main reasons people give for dropping their membership or not joining is that dues are too high.
- Any aspect of the dues structure and join or renewal process is described as confusing, frustrating, stressful, or challenging.

When is the right time to raise dues?

When the association is stable and healthy and well-positioned for growth. When member engagement is high, retention is up, and the association offers must-have membership with significant ROI. When the dues diligence is complete, and the association can tell its story and raise dues to expand benefits and better serve members.

When the intention is right and the positioning is right, the time will be right for a change.

WHO ON OUR TEAM SHOULD BE RESPONSIBLE FOR MEMBERSHIP STRATEGY?

From recruitment to service, recognition, and retention, there is much debate about who is ultimately responsible for setting and overseeing the membership strategy. There's also a considerable amount of back-burning and hot-potato-tossing. By this I mean there are associations that either don't have a membership strategy in place or don't have anyone appointed to the role of membership. Then, when decline occurs, there's a lot of finger-pointing, uncertainty, and confusion.

This is partly because membership associations haven't needed to rely heavily on strategy in the past. People joined. They stayed. There wasn't a lot of pushback, change in demand, market shifts, competition, technological advancements, or innovation.

Membership strategy is necessary to navigate this new norm. It's not something to leave unsupervised or up to chance. To succeed, several factors need to be modernized and addressed, including the prioritization of membership strategy and the appointment of people to oversee it.

For starters, the top tier of association org charts usually looks something like this:

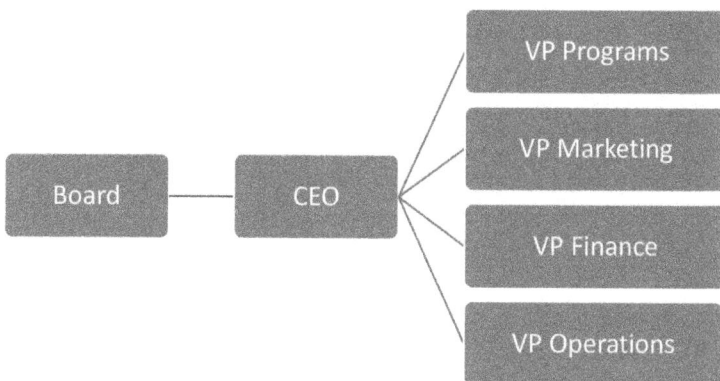

Where is membership in this structure? It's not a designated role at the executive level, and if it's just assumed membership will be a consideration within each of these other roles, the association risks experiencing inefficiencies or loss of focus.

The structure needs to be revamped. Consider whether the outcomes would be different if the association was designed to be member centric.

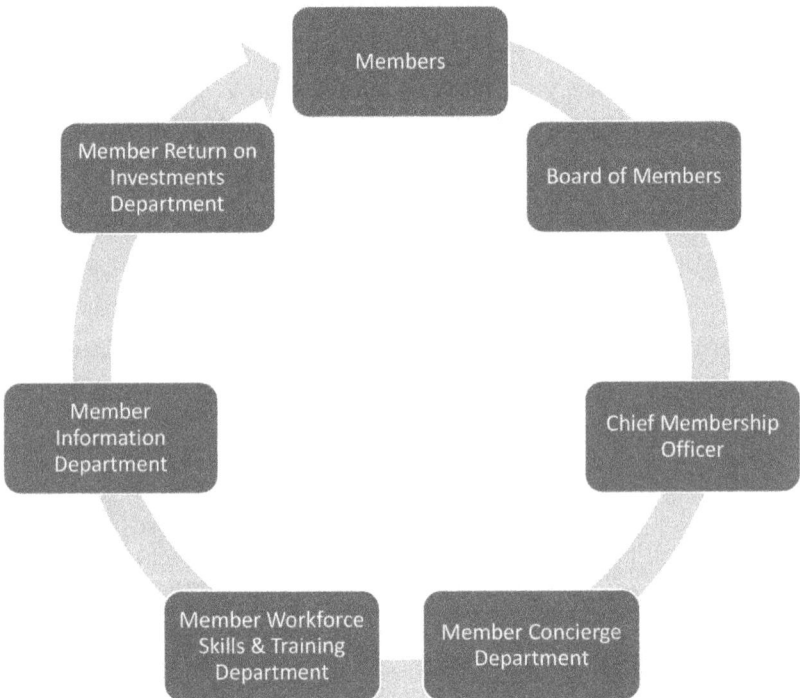

What does being truly member centric look like in terms of governance and operations?

Picture this:

- The Board of Members is a diverse representation of the membership, inspired to lead the organization with a future-focused, member-centric mindset.
- A Chief Membership Officer is hyper-focused on membership service, recognition, and growth.
- The Member Concierge Department is responsible for creating the best membership experiences and recognition programs and culling the best member benefits.
- The Member Skills & Training Department equips members with top-tier professional training, and career-readiness, mentoring, and job-shadowing programs for students and young professionals.
- The Member Information Department disseminates valuable research, publications, and video broadcasts to members.
- The Member Investments Department handles the financial well-being of the association, in addition to tracking and reporting on membership ROI.

If this was the case, the membership strategy would be a collective effort, with every department contributing their part, overseeing their individual areas of expertise, and tracking progress. All the effort and focus would be on the members and success would undoubtedly follow.

MEMBERSHIP ISN'T CEREAL

Like a bad infomercial, there are many companies out there schlepping membership strategy as a quick fix. If I had a buzzer to hit in response to every wrong answer, I would hit it after each of these remarks:

Want to grow membership? Use social media! (Buzz!)

Host more events! (Buzz!)

Purchase our community-building software! (Buzz!)

Launch a membership drive! Do a direct mail campaign! Make more phone calls! (Buzz! Buzz! And buzz!)

Be wary of any consultant or company that promises a quick fix in the absence of in-depth analysis and experienced membership strategy development. The decision to join and engage is steeped in emotion and reasoning.

Membership isn't a box of cereal. Far from it. Attempts to tweak pricing, packaging, and promotion will be ineffective at curbing decline or driving growth.

The only way to engage members is to be member-centric, putting their needs and interests first.

CHAPTER 2: DISCUSSION GUIDE

Reflect and respond. Write your answers in the book or download the play-book online and fill it out. Share and discuss with others in the association.

Which of the following questions continuously pop up in your association? Check all that apply.

- ☐ What's our value proposition?
- ☐ How do I know if members are engaged?
- ☐ Why won't young professionals join?
- ☐ What incentives should we use to recruit new members?
- ☐ When is the right time to raise dues?
- ☐ When should we expand our membership market?
- ☐ Who on our team should be responsible for membership strategy?

Based on what you learned in this chapter, what do you consider the top three priorities? What are the action steps the association can take immediately to effectively answer these questions and turn the obstacles into opportunities?

1.

_____

_____

_____

2.

_____

_____

What inspires you when thinking about creating a member-centric org chart?

_____

_____

_____

_____

_____

_____

What concerns you when thinking about creating a member-centric org chart?

_____

_____

_____

_____

_____

After reading this chapter, where did you identify opportunities for improvement? In your opinion, what immediate changes are needed to place the association on a member-centric path?

_____

_____

_____

_____

_____

*Homework:

During the next 30 days, brainstorm ways the association could transition to the Invited-Belong-Participate-Appreciate Cycle to Engagement, which relies heavily on outreach, opportunity, and recognition. Consider the following questions. Ask your association colleagues to do the same. Then, at the end of 30 days, set aside time as a team to share your findings with one another.

- Invited: Who should the association be targeting and inviting to join? What are some creative or meaningful ways the association could extend invites to prospective members?
- Belong: What actions can the association take to successfully onboard, serve, wow, inform, or inspire new and prospective members?
- Participate: What volunteer opportunities could the association offer to new members seeking to immediately get connected and involved?
- Appreciate: What are some of the ways our association can regularly thank and recognize members for their volunteerism?

CHAPTER 3

MEMBERS FIRST

Thinking it is enough for the association to provide members access to something they want and need is not fully understanding what belonging is or what members are seeking from the membership experience.

I was seated in the office building of an international membership association. The walls were lined with historic photos, awards, and memorabilia, and the CEO, seated opposite me at a large mahogany conference table, was shocked by the words that had just come out of my mouth.

I had just told him the membership association didn't appear to be in the business of membership.

Hired to conduct research and provide strategic guidance to the organization, my firm was charged with identifying why membership was declining. Upon further review, it became clear this was happening because membership wasn't the priority.

How is it possible membership isn't the priority in a membership organization? It happens more often than association leaders realize.

In this instance, most of the association's resources were focused on producing events and advertising campaigns. There was an intense focus on garnering support for and serving the industry in its entirety. Furthermore, non-members had access to nearly everything members had access to, so membership had lost its value.

When there isn't a clear return on investment—dues for access, goods, or services—it's hard to categorize the dues transaction as anything other than a donation.

In the decisions and actions of the association, membership was no longer the priority, which was evident in the sentiments members shared via surveys and interviews. By and large, members felt neglected and concluded they weren't receiving a return on their due investments. Nonetheless, when I told the CEO that day the organization wasn't engaging members because the organization wasn't prioritizing members, the news came as quite a shock.

It starts out with the best intentions. Leadership teams pursue other interests or causes, making the mistake of believing these efforts will result in growth in revenues, market share, and ultimately membership. But when service to members and return on investment to members is backburnered to focus elsewhere, the association often ends up losing what it was hoping to gain.

Most of us are familiar with the adage, "Where your time and money is, so is your heart." The same is true for membership organizations. Listed in the chart below are examples of how associations shift focus, prioritizing time and money in areas that negatively impact membership.

When this happens	The priority is	Which creates a challenge because
Considerable time and resources are directed toward the planning of conferences and events.	Event Planning	The association's brand becomes synonymous with events and the association's financial stability relies heavily on the revenues generated by events. Members begin to question the value a membership provides, and the cost to attend events competes with the cost of membership. People pay to attend certain conferences as their budgets and schedules allow but won't pay to join the association. Cash flow ebbs and flows, reliant on event attendance.
The association invests resources and effort into lobbying and excels at government relations but struggles to be responsive to the needs of members and build relationships with them.	Advocacy	Advocacy isn't a member benefit. People benefit from the association's advocacy efforts, whether they are a member or not. A heavy emphasis on advocacy leads to discontent among members, who expect the investment in advocacy to deliver continual wins. In the day-to-day, they question the return on investment and whether the association is there to help them.

When this happens	The priority is	Which creates a challenge because
The association isn't responsive to or representative of the entire membership community. These associations struggle to retain staff or keep members engaged. On the other hand, the board is highly regarded, respected, and engaged.	Governance	Associations relying on hierarchical models tend to be most at-risk of aging out. These associations struggle to be open to new ideas and new people, which contributes to both staff turnover and membership decline.
The association launches publicity campaigns and public service initiatives or offers programs and services that equally benefit and serve non-members and members. There is little to no differentiation between members and non-members.	Non-Members	Being open and readily available to all dilutes the value of membership. When the association isn't responsive to or representative of the entire membership community, these associations struggle to retain staff or keep members engaged. On the other hand, the board is highly regarded, respected, and engaged.

When members aren't the priority, the association puts itself at risk. Membership decline leads to revenue decline and other unwanted side effects. It's also difficult for an association to bounce back from these losses because the organization's brand changes and trust within the membership community deteriorates.

Membership can't be a priority unless the association is designed to function that way. This means membership is central to all the association does—from how the association is governed and decisions are made, to how the team is trained, what messages are sent out, and where the money is spent.

In my years of experience working for and with associations, one stands out as being exceptional in terms of being member-centric: Nexstar Network.

I was first introduced to Nexstar when I was invited to present at their annual conference, Super Meeting. If you took an extended family reunion and mixed it with the infamous footage of screaming fans at a Beatles conference, you'd have a fairly accurate portrayal of the Super Meeting.

Walking into the event was a memorable moment. It wasn't just the gobos, red carpet, and upbeat music that gave it that *je ne sais quoi*. As I watched people interact, it was striking how incredibly excited people were to be there and to be in community with one another.

What was Nexstar, an association for home service contractors, doing to foster this kind of enthusiasm and relationship-building? I wanted to know. Shortly thereafter, I interviewed a Nexstar executive and featured the association in my book, *Knowing Y*.

I've continued to follow the organization's success, which can be boiled down to one key point of differentiation: Nexstar puts members first. In fact, the association's mission and chief guiding principle is M1, which stands for Members First.

For this book, I revisited Nexstar and interviewed the organization's CEO. As you read their story, consider how the member-centric approach contributed to the association's success.

THE M1 METHODOLOGY

Founded in 1992, Nexstar Network represents independent home services contractors in plumbing, heating, air conditioning, and electrical trades. The association was founded to further the success of these companies, offering access to business training, leadership training, proven business systems, and dedicated business coaching.

Nexstar is a member-owned, for-profit organization, so members are referred to as shareholders, and every dollar of profit is returned to the members in the form of goods and services. The association has a governing board of members representing both small businesses and large businesses. Nexstar provides access to industry-specific subject matter expertise, including access to personalized coaching, in-depth training, and strategic vendor relationships. Upon joining, Nexstar member companies are assigned business, marketing, call center, finance, recruiting, sales, inventory, and technical training coaches. This individualized coaching provides a support system for members, helping them build a plan for success and achieve it. In addition, the association provides access to 150 partners, and members receive quarterly rebates for using these services, which they can apply toward their dues.

According to Julian Scadden, CEO, the unwavering focus on serving members is critical to the organization's success. Rather than contemplate expansion into other industries—something Nexstar has repeatedly been asked to do—the association remains focused on its mission, continually expanding to better serve members.

At Nexstar, this dedication to members is known as M1, Members First, which is the association's first guiding principle. M1 means going above and beyond to serve the members. There are many ways in which this guiding principle influences Nexstar's culture. Scadden highlighted the following two: being responsive with member communication and managing the members' money in a trustworthy, responsible way.

In terms of communication, staff are trained in hypothetical situations such as this one: *You receive three emails close to the end of the workday—one from the CEO, one from a work colleague, and one from a member. Which one do you respond to?* Staff are trained to respond to members first. "Everyone else can wait until tomorrow," Scadden explained.

This is M1.

In terms of finances, Nexstar streamlines expenses to prioritize the member experience. For example, the staff doesn't fly first class or book suites when they travel. Rather, the team is responsible for the success of their member businesses and ensuring members receive financial return for their dues. The focus on members is everywhere, including the Nexstar office, which features a designated bulletin board where staff posts notes and compliments to one another to draw attention to how they are caring for members.

M1 is the first guiding principle, and Nexstar's other principles support it:

- *Live business excellence.*
  The association was founded to teach its member companies best practices, so Nexstar itself strives to be a top-performing, best-practice organization.

- *Culture of caring and no enabling.*
  "Enabling environments allow people to give less than their best while someone else steps in and covers for them," Scadden explained. Nexstar fosters a caring environment, helping team members when they face challenges, and holding them accountable for their actions and decisions.

- *Bring more energy to work than you take.*
  Nexstar fosters a culture of positivity, problem-solving, and a path-to-yes mentality. Negativity, complaining, or other prac-

tices which "suck the energy out of the room" aren't tolerated, Scadden said.

- *Bad news early, good news often.*
  To have a great organization, staff must encourage and trust one another. Mistakes are shared right away. Accolades and gratitude are expressed often.

- *See it, say it directly and with respect.*
  The entire team holds one another accountable. Staff are trained on how to address conflict and initiate conversations without judgment or blame.

All Nexstar's guiding principles are prominently posted on artwork throughout the office, and employees are trained on each principle and why it's important to the Nexstar culture. The goal is to inform and empower employees so that during a critical decision-making moment, they can refer to the principles and make the right decision on the organization's behalf.

Annual benchmarking surveys indicate 89 percent of Nexstar's employees are highly engaged, in comparison with the national average of 64 percent. Likewise, members are also highly engaged. Nexstar boasts a 98 percent retention rate. Scadden credits the M1 model. At Nexstar, staff and members alike are invested in building and advancing the community, he explained. It's a shared ownership that forges strong ties throughout the entire organization.

Rather than just be content with this success rate, Nexstar continually measures engagement to ensure the organization stays at peak performance. The member engagement score is calculated by 19 factors, which are products, programs, and services that Nexstar has identified as providing valuable returns. The more a member participates, the higher the engagement score. Members receive a report on their annual engagement scores, and scores are also posted on member name badges at events. This spurs conversations, competitiveness, and a desire among members to get even more involved.

The organization has studied member participation alongside financial returns. Nexstar has proved membership grows a company's revenues by two or three times every year when members actively participate (78 percent or higher participation scores).

At a $30,000 initiation fee and $12,000 in annual dues thereafter, the price to join Nexstar is high, but so are the returns. "These businesses are deciding to invest in Nexstar rather than purchase new truck wraps, uniforms, or computers. They say, 'If I give the dues to Nexstar, it will bring me more return,'" Scadden said.

Nexstar recently increased the size of its team and moved from an office above a sub shop to the 21st floor of a skyscraper. Scadden said being on the 21st floor makes everyone feel they are on a new level professionally because of being a part of Nexstar.

The new office space included the addition of a large training center. Now, employees observe member trainings, regularly meet and interact with members, and gain a greater appreciation for the work Nexstar does and the people the organization represents.

Nexstar has achieved a high level of staff engagement and membership engagement by remaining solely focused on its mission as an M1 organization, and growth has been realized throughout the entire organization. In the past seven years,

- Membership doubled, from 500 members to over 1,000
- Staff size increased from 35 employees to 100
- The number of member trainings tripled, expanding from 65 classes per year to over 200
- Coaching services expanded, and Nexstar is now home to 65 coaches specializing in everything from business strategy to customer service and digital marketing

Putting members first has led to greater success for Nexstar Network.

OBSTACLES TO GROWTH

What about the Nexstar story inspired you? What about it felt daunting or impossible to achieve?

According to research, members join associations when they believe the association can help them solve a problem. And members will renew when the problem has been solved (or they believe the association is making a sincere effort to solve it) *and* they feel a sense of belonging.

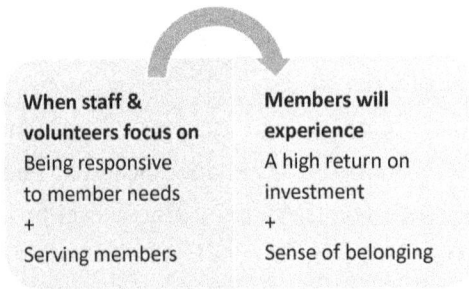

When staff & volunteers focus on	Members will experience
Being responsive to member needs	A high return on investment
+	+
Serving members	Sense of belonging

Membership growth relies entirely on an association's ability to solve problems and create a sense of community. The formula is straightforward. It isn't complex or difficult to understand, so why isn't every association member centric in their thinking and deliverables?

In my research of and work with associations, I've learned there are four core obstacles internally that prevent associations from putting members first:

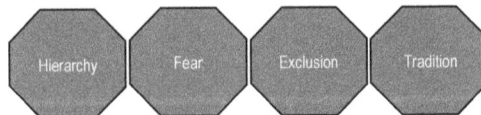

Hierarchy   Fear   Exclusion   Tradition

HIERARCHY

Let's start at the top. In recent years, the effectiveness of leadership has been called into question. How organizations lead, who is given the opportunity to lead, and what they are leading toward is evolving.

In the 20th century workplace, leadership was a role that had to be earned over time and came with its perks—a large office, great benefits, high salary. Work your way up the ladder, then reap the benefits. For some leaders, one such benefit was sitting on a board of directors, a prestigious role usually reserved for the most experienced executives. Now we live in a world in transition. Society shifted from a model that was utilized for centuries with minor adaptations to a model that is constantly changing, unpredictable, and sometimes unfamiliar. Change is happening faster than ever, which means associations need to rethink their hierarchical leadership models.

To be effective in establishing a path for growth, relevance, and success, boards of directors and volunteer leaders need to be

✓ Closely tied to the association's mission
✓ Closely tied to the association's members
✓ Open to change; and
✓ Cognitively diverse

Still today, there are many associations relying on the hierarchical leadership model, reserving leadership roles for those with executive-level jobs or people who have been dedicated members for many years.

Associations need to reconsider leadership criteria for board members. It doesn't matter if a leader has a top-notch education, knowledge, and great experience. If they don't care about the association's mission and members, they aren't the right fit.

When I work on membership strategy with a client, one question I always ask is: Who are some of your biggest fans—people who are especially positive, inspired, and passionate about the association's future success? I've asked many organizations this same question, and rarely are board members the first people to pop to mind. This is an alarming discovery, further pointing to the need to retire the hierarchical leadership model.

In a hierarchy, leaders are a homogenous, like-minded group of people. When everyone is around the same age or comes from the same backgrounds, they cannot understand or represent the diverse needs of the membership community. They also cannot identify trends or predict change. This model hinders vision and passion—the two leadership traits associations most need access to right now.

Leadership today isn't about power or titles earned. It isn't defined by experience or age. Rather, leadership is associated with the ability to determine vision, continually moving an organization into the future and toward greater relevance.

With this purpose in mind, leaders also need to have the right mindset.

When I authored the book *Talent Generation: How Visionary Organizations are Redefining Work and Achieving Greater Success* (2017), I spent several years researching organizations with high success rates, defined as organizations that had maintained both high profitability and high employee engagement. My research revealed the same traits were prevalent among all the leaders.

Each leader:

- Felt passionate toward the mission and deeply cared for the people working in the organization.
- Led with humility and demonstrated a willingness to learn.
- Acted with urgency, was decisive, and kept the organization focused on reaching key goals.

Returning to the question of who the most passionate people are in the association, my research has revealed passion is missing from association boards of directors. Passion typically exists in a close relationship with humility and urgency, so without it, organizations struggle to get very far, very fast.

Passionate leaders are curious, connected, desire to serve others, and want to do the best work possible. They are visionary, and people naturally follow them because they ooze enthusiasm and inspire excellence. Passion is the differentiator. To successfully compete in a rapidly changing market, associations need leaders who are passionate about building a better experience and community for members.

Hierarchy was a defining part of history, leading the way for centuries. But here and now, it's holding progress back, side-lining vision and passion, and preventing associations from being membercentric. The leadership should reflect the diverse needs and interests of the membership community in its entirety, which means it's time to retire the homogenous, high-ranking hierarchical leadership model of the past.

FEAR

We've all known leaders who ignored change to the point of feeling calm and confident, even while watching their organizations decline and spiral out of control. In these situations, apathy, over-confidence, and the delusion that "it will change back" prevent leaders from fully comprehending the severity of a crisis or responding to change.

Why does this happen? Blame brain science and board make-up.

For all of us, the fear of change is a scientifically proven obstacle. When we encounter change, it literally lights up the prefrontal cortex in our brains. Initially, we feel excitement toward the concept of change. The prefrontal cortex is agile, and we quickly compute options for reacting to the change. However, the prefrontal cortex's capacity is limited. It can deal comfortably with new concepts for only a short period. After that, we experience a physiological sense of discomfort—usually fatigue or anger. We experience this because the prefrontal cortex is tightly linked to the emotional center of the brain, the amygdala, which controls our fight-or-flight response.

Ultimately, doing what we know makes us feel better. It's why we resist change. Our brains prefer a comfortable, predictable, familiar path.

The fear of change is further nurtured by the hierarchical organizational structure.

Board leadership usually goes something like this: Board members are appointed to lead for a limited time, and the role is positioned as one of prominence, achievement, and cause for celebration. Board members are placed in the spotlight, sworn in or sign an oath, continually reminded of their responsibility to the organization, and urged to leave a legacy.

All things considered, is it any surprise fears of change or failure kick in?

People want to feel their time in leadership yields a successful outcome for the organization. No board member wants to make a decision that could negatively alter the fate of the organization. Rather than try something new or risk rocking the boat, it's comforting and reassuring to stay on course and do more of the same. This is how entire organizations can end up turning a blind eye to the need for change.

The same process exists among staff, too. Most organizations are designed to reward teams for doing their work rather than achieving results. Do your job and get an annual pay raise. This means teams are rewarded for continuing to do more of the same, further contributing to the fear of change and trying something new or different.

Thankfully, there is an antidote to the fear of change. Collaboration.

It's scientifically proven. We're less likely to respond with fight-or-flight when we're supported by, and in community with, other people. Teamwork eases fears, making it possible to adapt and accomplish change.

Teamwork inspires innovation and empathy. Even better, teams achieve higher performance when they are cognitively diverse, bringing together people representing different backgrounds, ages, skillsets, and experiences. Cognitive diversity is the opposite of the homogenous teams common in hierarchical leadership models, and it is critical to building a relevant, sustainable membership community.

We rarely stop to think about it, but teambuilding is a new, unexplored concept in our workplaces and associations. Throughout most of the 20th century, children were taught to work independently, with only the occasional team project thrown into the curriculum. Likewise, workplaces were almost entirely focused on individual achievements and paths to success, further evident in the language used and comments like "work your way up the ladder" and "pay your dues."

The 21st century introduced a greater emphasis on group activities, partly because of advancements in technology and partly because of shifts in parenting.

Helicopter parenting emerged, a term used to describe a social shift to protect children. In fact, the Millennial generation would become the most protected, supervised, and provided for generation in history. Growing up in a close relationship with parents and coaches would initiate a shift from working independently or in silos to teamwork, mentoring, and collaboration. And growing up with technology ushered in new team-centric opportunities, like social networking and online gaming, and surges in innovation and teams launching business start-ups.

It used to be teamwork was reserved for specific tasks and occasions, which is why the concept of team building and teamwork doesn't always come naturally. It's a new concept, but it's one we need to get comfortable with, and fast. This is the way the market is headed, plus research proves it really is teamwork that makes the dream work.

Collaboration eases our fears of change and failure, and cognitive diversity generates better results. Both are needed to combat the fears that hold associations back, and both support an association's efforts to build a relevant, representative, and inclusive community.

Collaboration is member centric. Fear is not.

EXCLUSION

It seems contradictory and unlikely that members of a membership organization would feel like they don't belong. However, many organizations are struggling to foster a sense of belonging among members, and have been for quite some time. We know this to be true because associations and employers alike have reported declining levels of member and employee engagement in recent years.

Belonging transitioned in the 1990s. From workplaces to membership associations, the same trend was realized and reported on by national media: Young people were notably less likely to join, stay, engage, and renew. Young people were less likely to feel like they belong.

Belonging is sometimes interpreted to mean one thing and one thing only: access. As in: Members pay dues to have access to association resources and community. They pay dues to belong. This isn't an accurate representation of belonging or why associations were founded.

Membership associations were established to be communities of support and representation for people with shared needs, interests, values, and ideas. The intent was never to create something transactional, positioning associations as little more than a storefront.

From Netflix to American Express and Sam's Club, the word membership is used. During the past two decades, more corporations have utilized the term to describe a subscription offer that provides the subscriber (member) access to discounts, products, or services. One author even published a book, *The Membership Economy*, about the rise in subscription-based business models.

But membership isn't a product. It's not transactional, and certainly not limited to access. As I explained with the cereal scenario in Chapter 2, membership is relationship based. When you join, you are deciding to be a part of a community and to be in a relationship with that community.

And relationships are two-way streets. Associations must do their part to contribute.

Associations aren't storefronts for members to visit as needed. Thinking it is enough for the association to provide members access to something they want and need is not fully understanding what belonging is or what members are seeking from the membership experience.

Belonging means two things: ownership and a secure relationship. For members to feel engaged, they must have

- The opportunity to make a meaningful difference in the association, and
- Connectivity to, and trust in, the association's leadership, mission, and other people in the organization

Belonging doesn't come from access alone. It's not on demand. The decision to join doesn't automatically lead to feelings of engagement, positivity, or belonging.

Furthermore, belonging will be limited to a small group of people in the membership community when the membership organization limits its relationship-building efforts to a small group of people.

Associations often lament there are small pockets of people who are engaged in their organizations and that extending beyond that pocket has proven to be a difficult, if not impossible, feat. In these cases, I always turn it back to the definition of belonging and the need for ownership and a secure relationship. Is the association creating pathways so all members can experience these two things? Often, the answer is no.

Providing access to a resource or community is not enough. Associations must be intentional about creating places of belonging for their members—*all* members.

It's imperative that your association doesn't get stuck in the past, allowing history to dictate its future. In the past, it was the norm to have hierarchical structures and only focus on engagement at the leadership level. In the past, it was a social expectation for people to join associations. Those social constructs no longer exist.

Today, community-building is literally about community and finding ways to bring every member an opportunity to connect, learn, lead, and make a difference. Today, community-building doesn't happen without belonging.

When entire segments of the membership community feel like they don't belong, disengagement and decline inevitably follow. Exclusion prevents associations from being member-centric. Associations must make room for everyone to belong.

TRADITION

I was in a meeting with an association client, and we were celebrating the team's accomplishments and membership growth. The conversation was light and animated. Then, I recommended they celebrate some of their accomplishments at the next board meeting. The conversation came to a screeching halt as a stunned silence fell over the room.

Finally, the association's CEO spoke up. "You think we should celebrate with the board?"

"Absolutely," I said. "The board should know what you're accomplishing, and it's an opportunity to celebrate and do something fun."

"Something fun?"

"Yes! Something fun," I said. Then I asked, "When is the last time you did something fun in the association?"

Again, there was a stunned silence. "I don't remember ever doing anything fun with the board," the CEO answered.

After further conversation, it became clear the association staff was afraid to stray from tradition. Historically, board meetings at this association were formal affairs, approached with considerable reverence and pomp and circumstance. I will not advocate for the curtailing of traditions in this book, but I will advocate for their review. It's important to take stock and ask whether traditions are creating positive momentum in the association or draining the energy out of it.

Creating sustainable, vibrant communities of belonging starts with assuring the organization is, in fact, a place where people want to be. Remember, tradition isn't relegated to a specific action, event, or occasion. Tradition can permeate the customs, beliefs, and attitudes that exist in your association. When traditions interfere with the membership experience, creating an organization void of enjoyment, celebration, or belonging, people will be less likely to want to spend their valuable resources or time on membership.

What I have learned through research is that success abounds when associations are obsessed with serving, wowing, inspiring, and informing the members. When tradition sets the tone, the best interests of members take a backseat, and it becomes increasingly difficult for an organization to engage members or grow.

Tradition prevents associations from being member-centric. Associations must innovate to survive.

MEMBERSHIP IS EVERYTHING

The phrase "What got you here won't get you there" sums up the situation perfectly. The membership models of the past are no longer sustainable. Assuming membership can stay the course in a world that's constantly changing is like pouring a full glass of milk and placing it on the floor of a tilt-a-whirl. Eventually, the momentum is too much.

The glass tips, shatters, and the milk spills everywhere. The concept you started with is no longer contained and spirals out of control.

The same effect is happening within membership organizations. They lost sight of what's important and became fragile amid continuous change, slowly but steadily losing control of something they tried so hard to preserve. They are at the tipping point, and there is only one thing they can do to prevent the organization from breaking.

Put members first. Become a must-have, member-centric membership organization. M1. 24/7. 365 days a year.

The first time I wrote about Nexstar Network was in 2015 for my book, *Knowing Y: Engage the Next Generation Now.* I toured the Nexstar offices and interviewed staff. I remember it well, especially the part when an employee turned to me and said, "Our members trump everything. If you don't really care about your members, you don't have an association. Membership is everything."

Is membership *everything* in your association? If the organization has experienced persistent fluctuations in participation, membership, or revenues, the answer is likely no.

When membership is everything, the association carefully considers how every decision, action, and experience affects the members. When membership is everything, membership is everyone's job. It is the responsibility of staff and volunteers to decide and take actions with the care of the members as the chief priority. When membership is everything, that's all that matters.

| Member-Centric Organizations | Non-Member-Centric Organizations |

Growth increases

Risk declines

Growth declines

Risk increases

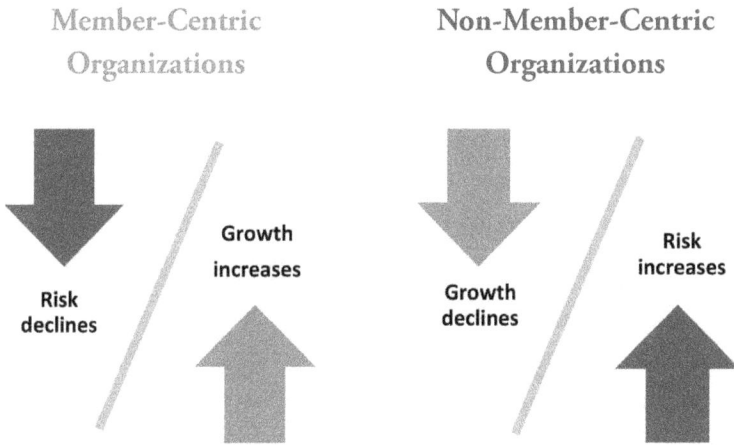

Remaining laser-focused on mission and who and what matters most keeps organizations relevant and stable, even during change. When associations are in close relationship with their members, two things happen:

1. Member engagement goes up, which drives demand and positions the association for sustained revenues and growth.
2. The risk of disengagement and decline go down, bringing sustained revenues and allowing the association to focus on mission, community-building, and the member experience.

Membership organizations were created to be close-knit communities of representation and service, but change shifted many of them into survival mode. Rather than double-down on helping members, associations turned to other sources of revenue and opportunity and began to backburner membership altogether. This fractured the relationship they had with members, and associations desperately need to find their way back.

Being closely aligned with and responsive to the changing needs and interests of members is the only way forward. Creating something that's important, necessary, and completely attuned to members will align the association to a people-first, future-focused strategy.

When this happens, the association will no longer consider itself at risk because decline and disengagement will no longer be threats. No matter what the tilt-a-whirl throws at your organization, it will remain entirely intact and unaffected because the focus isn't on the change—it's on the members and being the most valuable and important resource the association can possibly be to them.

For any membership organization seeking to prosper and grow, M1 must be priority number one. For the members, by the members, as it was originally intended to be. M1 is the only solution.

CHAPTER 3: DISCUSSION GUIDE

Reflect and respond. Write your answers in the book or download the playbook online and fill it out. Share and discuss with others in the association.

Which of the following are currently preventing your association from being member- centric? Check all that apply.

- ☐ Hierarchy
- ☐ Fear
- ☐ Exclusion
- ☐ Tradition

Who are some of the association's biggest fans—people who are especially positive, inspired, and passionate about the association's future success?

_____

_____

_____

_____

_____

How could the association empower its fan base, increasing their involvement and bringing their voices to the forefront?

_____

_____

_____

_____

_____

What inspires you when thinking about creating an M1 organization?

_____

_____

_____

_____

_____

What concerns you when thinking about creating an M1 organization?

_____

_____

_____

_____

_____

After reading this chapter, where did you identify opportunities for improvement? What immediate changes are needed to place the association on a member-centric path?

_____

_____

_____

_____

_____

*Homework:

During the next 30 days, brainstorm ways the association could eliminate the obstacles to growth and begin creating a member-centric organization. Consider the following questions. Ask your association colleagues to do the same. Then, at the end of 30 days, set aside time as a team to share your findings with one another.

- Hierarchy: What changes need to happen to ensure the association empowers and engages leaders who have passion and vision?
- Fear: What changes need to happen to ensure the association's leadership is cognitively diverse?
- Exclusion: What changes would help foster belonging, giving every member the opportunity to learn, lead, and make a difference?
- Tradition: Which traditions interfere with the membership experience? What changes would create an organization renowned for its culture of joy, celebration, and belonging?

*Understanding what different segments of your audience
need and value and accepting these values shift over time
are critical to an association's long-term success.*

KNOW YOUR VALUE

There's a comic strip that shows a man, dressed in a fancy suit, taking a helicopter to a mountaintop. He meets a guru who is looking relaxed and serene, sitting near a cave. The man looks down at the guru and says, "What is the meaning of life? But make it quick—I've got an important meeting in half an hour."

Since the beginning of time, philosophers, comedians, religious leaders, and many others have pondered the meaning-of-life question. *Why are we here? What is our purpose? What does it all mean?*

In the comic, it's obvious the businessman is missing it. He's wealthy and successful, but he's not taking time to be in the moment, enjoy simple pleasures, or focus on the truly important things. His values are clearly misaligned.

Much like the meaning-of-life question, in recent years membership organizations have puzzled over their value propositions, trying to understand why the market stopped buying what they're offering. *Why are we here? What is our purpose? What does it all mean?* And much like the cartoon, I've observed the focus is on the wrong things. What associations are offering isn't what members want. The values are misaligned.

Values are very influential. Values motivate our decisions and behaviors, including where we work, what products we buy, and with whom we choose to spend our time. Undoubtedly, when an association can pinpoint what members value, it will better understand what switches on the decision to join, buy, or participate.

However, there are many misunderstandings about what values are, how they are formed, and why they matter. Before your association can successfully identify its value proposition, we first need to clearly understand how values are developed, why they are changing, and the various ways values influence membership engagement.

First things first: What are values, and where do they come from?

VALUES ARE INFLUENCED BY SOCIAL CHANGE

The Great Depression began in August 1929 in the United States and spread throughout the world. The crisis lasted a decade, becoming the longest and deepest financial downturn in the modern economy. Industrial production plummeted. Unemployment soared. People suffered.

My mother was born in the final years of the Depression. It left a lasting impression on her. She told stories of seeing families wander the streets, looking for food or shelter. She remembered rationing food, sewing her own clothes, and saving rainwater.

If you've ever known someone who grew up during this era, you know how much they valued their homes, the consistency of a paycheck, and how difficult it could be to throw something away. Impacted by years of need during their childhoods, many people in the Silent Generation worked long hours and scrimped and saved to provide a better future for their children.

Values are shaped during childhood and early adolescence and are influenced by socializing agents, which influence our behaviors, norms, and values. Significant people and circumstances, media, school, culture, and religion are all socializing agents, and all are influenced in part by what's happening in society at a given time.

There are people who believe socializing agents have little to do with value development. To my horror, I recently read an article in which the author alleged values are tied to your alcoholic drink of choice. This is absurd!

Socializing agents influence value development, just as the Depression influenced my mother's generation, and World War II and other significant events influenced successive generations of youth.

A more recent example is the outbreak of COVID-19. The event affected people of all ages, but for children and teens in the early stages of brain development and value development, the experience was defining.

For example, the National Library of Medicine reported that in comparison to adults, youth experiencing pandemic and quarantine experienced higher levels of separation, grief, loss, acute stress, anxiety, and depression. In addition, the experience impacted youth earnings and employment, food security, and access to healthcare and foundational learning.

Undoubtedly, as this generation moves into adulthood, they will value security, safety, predictability, positivity, and belonging.

Values shift from generation to generation because society is constantly shifting and evolving. As a result, association executives need to pay close attention to how the youth of today are impacted by social change and how these changes influence value development. This is one of the best ways to anticipate shifts in value proposition.

Problems arise when membership organizations become stagnant and don't take the time to survey, explore, or discuss the changing needs of their audience. Understanding what different segments of your audience need and value and accepting that these values shift over time are critical to an association's long-term success.

VALUES ARE DEVELOPED DURING CHILDHOOD

In 1982, the home computer arrived, and this changed everything about the way people lived, communicated, and worked. Educators and demographers noticed a significant shift in values in the years that followed.

On annual basic needs assessments, school-age children started to rank access to technology as equally, and sometimes more, valuable than access to oxygen and freedom. These initial findings both shocked and puzzled educators and psychologists, but it's since become an accepted norm.

If you were born after 1982, you have never known life without technology, and that has influenced your value development. You've always known an on-demand, virtual world driven by customization, instant gratification, mobility, flexibility, globalization, and personalization. It is not surprising that the generations born since 1982 expect employers and associations to value, use, and prioritize tech-based platforms and leverage the access, innovation, and features a technology-driven approach provides.

Yet, when the global pandemic hit in 2020, it became apparent the transition to technology was sorely lagging. It became common for leaders born prior to 1982 to say the pandemic forced their organizations online. For many, the shift to remote work and virtual events was a wake-up call because they suddenly realized they were out of their comfort zones, and their organizations were woefully behind and far from tech-savvy. Technology wasn't ingrained into their values systems. They didn't view it as a priority, so their initial response to tech-immersion was resistance.

Even then, many insisted the shift to technology was temporary, saying they couldn't wait to "get back to normal." Yet, for people born after 1982, having never known life without technology, the use of technology is considered normal.

It's a struggle when our values don't align. It creates conflict and gaps within associations and contributes to disengagement and decline. The situation worsens when there's an attempt to ignore or shift values. This mindset exists in comments like:

- We've always done it this way.
- You're going to have to just deal with it.
- When you question what we're doing, you're being disrespectful.
- Change takes time.

Shifts in society influence shifts in values, which introduce the need for organizations to expand their approach and modernize.

I'm often asked how associations can successfully engage young members and respond to their values while not alienating older generations of members. Let's take the emotional and personal out of that question and focus on facts.

- Fact: Engaging young people requires associations to modernize. When associations stop modernizing, they struggle to stay relevant and engage new people with new ideas.
- Fact: Eventually, members of all ages expect associations to modernize because society continually evolves and modernizes. As a result, new values are constantly emerging and end up influencing all of society. (This is known as Trickle-Up Effect.)
- Fact: Associations were founded to represent entire communities of people—not specific age groups. If the move to be inclusive of new people with new ideas is perceived as a threat to the association's current members, that's likely an indication the association isn't thinking or acting like a community-based organization. Rather, it's being governed like an exclusive club.

There's a key difference between values we are raised with and values we adjust to later in life. The values we're raised with are the values we go back to every time we feel stressed, anxious, or confused. We adapt to our surroundings as we mature, but those core values that were shaped during our childhoods and adolescence are consistent companions, often influencing our behaviors and attitudes without us even realizing it.

Therefore, attempts to build a relevant membership community are ineffective unless the leaders in those associations take the time to understand, and build relationships with, the many demographics of people represented within their community.

VALUES REQUIRE RESEARCH

Harley-Davidson is a true American icon with real brand cachet. The motorcycle company was founded in 1901, but it wasn't until the Baby Boomers (1946–1964) that sales skyrocketed. Boomers embraced the Harley bikes as totems of rebellion in the 1960s and 1970s and drove its growth in the ensuing decades.

However, in the 2010s, Harley made headlines as motorcycle sales launched into decline. Coasting on its success, it turns out the company neglected to prepare for change.

Harley Davidson's brand and sales depend disproportionately—almost exclusively—on middle-aged, Caucasian males. When decline began, the company tried to expand its reach to women, minorities, and younger generations with limited success.

Harley waited too long to engage other demographics and didn't research or respond to the changing values of the marketplace. The passing of the prominent Harley era is a reminder that not everything relevant to one generation will be relevant to the next.

Associations need to be careful not to follow suit.

☐ Check any of the boxes below that apply to your association's current state of operations:

☐ We haven't surveyed our members in the past two years.

☐ We don't survey members after their memberships have lapsed.

☐ Everyone on the board or with decision-making power in the association is over the age of 40.

☐ We must mostly guess what young people want since so few are involved.

☐ It's difficult to find the time to think about and plan for the future.

Like Harley-Davidson, your association may be at risk of aging out or becoming irrelevant if you can check any of the boxes above. Paying close attention to the changing needs and values of the marketplace is critical. This is not something an association can guess. Research is needed.

I've observed there are some strong sentiments that exist in associations when it comes to conducting surveys—specifically, a fear of over-surveying members. I've heard these worries expressed repeatedly, and it generally goes something like this: "We can't survey our members too often. They won't like it."

In a rapidly changing marketplace, research is necessary and important. And contrary to popular belief, people want to share their feedback, ideas, and experiences. Consider the rise in platforms asking for customer feedback and the high volume of people taking part. Nearly 60 percent of online shoppers refer to Google and Amazon reviews, and TripAdvisor is home to more than a billion reviews!

Surveys that are long and complex likely won't be well-received or generate much participation, but there are more effective ways to gather research, such as polls and one-question surveys. Or select a different group of ten members each month to have coffee with the CEO and share feedback. Or host a focus group with young professionals.

Research is taking the time to interact with and know your audience, but it's also taking the time to learn about your future audience. Read industry publications, browse TikTok, watch popular YouTube channels, and put yourself into the future figuratively and literally. Always be learning and observing people, trends, and youth culture. Set time aside for the staff and board to discuss what they've learned from these exercises.

Far too few organizations take the time to understand their audience and the values represented within, and *that's* why the market isn't buying what they're offering.

Want to find your organization's value? Start by valuing the opinions, insights, and values of your audience. Therein lies the answer.

VALUES AND MEMBERSHIP

Society shifts, values shift, so clearly the membership value proposition must also shift. The following graphic shows the various ways values ultimately influence a member's decision to join an association. The sections in purple represent what members themselves value, want, need, and expect from membership. The sections in orange represent what associations can create to align their cultures, systems, and processes with member values.

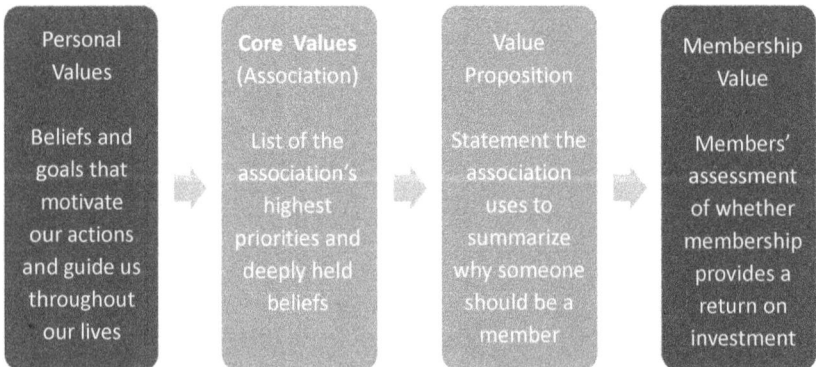

Personal Values	Core Values (Association)	Value Proposition	Membership Value
Beliefs and goals that motivate our actions and guide us throughout our lives	List of the association's highest priorities and deeply held beliefs	Statement the association uses to summarize why someone should be a member	Members' assessment of whether membership provides a return on investment

PERSONAL VALUES

I shared the story of my mother earlier in this chapter and some values prevalent among children born during the Great Depression. This is an example of personal values, which are developed during childhood and adolescence and are largely influenced by social norms and trends prominent during the time of our upbringing. As a result, generations of people raised during the same era will often share some of the same values.

Furthermore, the values formed during our early stages of brain development are the values we carry throughout our entire lives and resort to in times of challenge or crisis. Personal values can evolve as we age and as society changes, but they don't change.

Review the chart below for additional insights:

	Boomers	Gen X	Gen Y	Gen Z
Born	1946–1964	1965–1981	1982–1995	1996–2009
Defining Social Movement of that Era	Post-World War II and the Great Depression; people had a renewed sense of hope and confidence in the future, and there was a baby boom.	Number of working women and divorce rates increased. Most Xers were raised in single-parent or two-parent working households.	Largest generation in history globally came of age alongside a tech boom; increased access to media and information shifts parenting styles.	The era of global disruption began, marked by political conflict, terrorism, climate change, and increased awareness of social inequality.

Common Social Influences During Youth	Beatlemania Moon Landing JFK Assassination Woodstock Vietnam War Civil Rights	Women's Rights Watergate Latch-Key Kids Cable Television Live Aid Divorce	Computers September 11 School Shootings Great Recession Helicopter Parents Participation Awards	Wireless Technology Social Media Marriage Equality Political Controversy Pandemic Climate Change
Society's Expectation of Youth	Raised to pursue the American Dream of financial success	Raised to be self-sufficient and independent	Raised to be high-achievers and pursue advanced degrees	Raised to compete and contemplate their futures
Common Values	Loyalty Dedication Experience Results	Work-Life Balance Honesty Autonomy Trust	Collaboration Innovation Respect Return on Investment	Equality Mental Health Creativity Problem-Solving
What They Want from Membership	Opportunities to lead and leave a legacy	Opportunities to further their careers	Opportunities to access new skills and information	Opportunities to influence change

Our personal values are our convictions regarding what we believe is important and desirable. Personal values may include a status someone wants to achieve (i.e., healthy, successful, or financial security) or a desired characteristic or way of behaving (i.e., honest, positive, or charitable). To be clear, personal values aren't the same for everyone raised during the same time, but there are similarities because people raised during the same era have many of the same social experiences.

Personal values matter in membership because values affect the decisions people make, including whether to join an association. As the chart shows, values can differ by generation, and what they want from their membership experiences can also differ. Being mindful of and responsive to the shifts in personal values are keys to your association's ability to continually engage members.

CORE VALUES

Just as we develop values on a personal level, entire organizations and groups of people are navigated by their value systems, as well. Members are constantly getting a read on your organization's values and deciding whether their personal values align. From the website to how your association onboards members and conducts meetings, to how physical spaces are designed at events, and the symbols and jargon used—everything an association says and does reflects its core values.

Some organizations are better than others at clarifying and communicating their values. Whether they are formally outlined, the values are always present in how the organization makes decisions and the people in the organization communicate with one another. In fact, the values of the broader organization can influence a member's decision to join or stay engaged.

An example that comes to mind here is an experience I had with a former client. When the association hired me to develop a membership strategy for them, they were upfront about the decline they had been experiencing for several years. After further investigation, it became apparent that part of the problem stemmed from within their membership.

A few unhappy members—including some board members—started posting negative comments on the association's social media channels. Board meetings became settings for more toxic commentary and arguing. Like a bad virus, the negativity became contagious, infecting the entire association as more people jumped on the bandwagon, bad-mouthing the association and other members. Complaints were overwhelming staff, as were notices of members dropping their memberships. The staff was at a complete loss for how to curb a situation that had spiraled completely out of control.

This is an example of what researchers Dave Logan, Ph.D., John King, and Halee Fischer-Wright, M.D., identified as a tribe. This team of researchers engaged in a 10-year workplace study and discovered groups of people who share similar attitudes (which they called tribes) significantly influence organizational culture, either for better or for worse. While their research is specific to workplaces, their findings certainly apply to membership associations.

The researchers identified five types of tribes. More importantly, they proved that attitudes are contagious, and the tribe's attitudes determine an organization's success. Jumps in productivity and profitability occur when positive tribes are formed, whereas reduced morale and productivity, apathy, and decline are prominent in organizations that house negative tribes.

If you want to know what stage a tribe is in, simply listen to how members talk about the association and interact with one another. Shared language is the primary indicator of a tribe's presence and status. Where does your association place in the tribe structure?

Stage One

These tribes are distinguished by hostility and despair. People say things like:

- "This association is the worst."

- "I don't know why I continue to be a member."
- "What a waste of time and money."

Stage Two

These tribes are characterized by apathy. Members stop volunteering, resist innovation, and revel in their disengagement, saying things like:

- "Why bother? Nothing will ever change anyway."
- "I'm retiring soon. This will be someone else's problem."
- "I'm only here because my employer pays for my dues."
- "This is the way we've always done it."

Stage Three

These tribes are competitive, self-centered, and averse to collaboration. The most common words they use are "I," "me," and "my." For example:

- "I have a plan to turn this group around."
- "That doesn't work for me."
- "I've been here longer than you."
- "My idea is better."

Stage Four

In this stage, tribe members have a sense of shared values, willingly share knowledge, and collaborate. These tribes are focused on improving as well as competing with other associations. People in these tribes say:

- "We're growing faster/offer more/been around longer."
- "We're stronger/larger/better."
- "We're the best choice."

Stage Five

Tribes that attain this level are characterized by a sense of happiness and amazement. They are highly innovative and collaborative and have a can-do attitude. These tribes are mission centric and inspired, often saying:

- "I love this association. I'm so glad I decided to join."
- "Because I'm a member of this association, my career/life is better."
- "There's so much opportunity here. I'm so excited about this organization's future."
- "I tell everyone I know to join this association."

The researchers discovered Stage Five tribes outperformed Stage Four tribes, which outperform Stage Three, and so on. Attitudes matter.

In the example of the association given above where negativity was rampant, core values weren't identified. By neglecting to define and enforce organizational values, the association's values and culture became fair game for the loudest, most influential voice (or tribe) to define. Unfortunately, in that example, the loudest cohort was also the most negative. As the saying goes, misery loves company.

Membership surveys further indicated members weren't feeling aligned with the association's culture or values, especially members under the age of 40. Unfortunately, the association's staff was hesitant to interfere and approach the members who were contributing to the association's negative culture and downward momentum. There were widespread concerns about making an already bad situation even worse.

I advised the team to focus on the development of organizational values alongside a group of positive and engaged members. The intent was two-fold: 1) To empower an influential group of people to offset the toxic energy, and 2) To chart a course forward as a team.

The group started by addressing these important questions:

- What are the behaviors we see today that we want to stop?
- What are the behaviors we see today that we want to continue?
- What are the behaviors we aren't seeing today that we need for the future?

By identifying a list of core values, then developing a strategy to actively communicate those values, the association defined and successfully transitioned the association's culture. By making a statement about what the association stands for and believes, and rallying a group of people behind the effort, the association created positive momentum and the members acting outside of the defined parameters were called out by other members. The people standing to the wayside spoke up and have renewed confidence in the association's culture and community-building efforts—none of which was possible until the association defined its core values.

Some examples of core values are listed in the chart below:

ALS Association	International Coaching Federation	Entrepreneurs Organization
• Compassion • Integrity • Urgency	• Professionalism • Collaboration • Humanity • Equity	• Trust and Respect • Thirst for Learning • Think Big, Be Bold • Together We Grow
School Nutrition Association	American Institute of CPAs	National Association of Manufacturers
• Integrity • Inclusion • Collaboration • Commitment • Innovation • Courage	• Lifelong Learning • Competence • Integrity • Attuned to Broad Business Issues • Objectivity	• Free Enterprise • Competitiveness • Individual Liberty • Equal Opportunity

Values are essential to the creation of a healthy, focused association. Values provide a framework for success while reinforcing organization-wide ethics and a code of conduct. Like a compass, values serve as a point of reference, always guiding the association forward and keeping it aligned with its true north, even in times of change.

Values also have the capacity to renew an organization's culture. If your organization doesn't have core values identified, appoint a task force comprised of a diverse group of stakeholders and staff to commence work on the development of values. It's important that the task force includes both next-generation members and ideal members. This ensures the values resonate with students and young professionals because they are the association's next generation of members and only succession plan, as well as people who represent the ideal member— forward-thinking, positive, innovative, and enthusiastic.

Once identified, the values should be prominently placed on the association's website, in marketing materials, board materials, and even included within the social media code of conduct.

In the example of the association struggling to manage a toxic culture, the identification of core values was a critical first step toward transformation. After identifying and publicizing the values, staff and board members had private conversations with those members who weren't abiding by the values. Within a matter of weeks, the association's culture shifted. The membership community started holding each other accountable to, and responsible for, upholding the values. The negativity was silenced, and positivity and other voices surfaced. The staff marveled at the speed and significance of the shift. Shortly after making the change, the association observed a surge in membership, with a record number of people joining the association in a single month.

Organizational values provide a consistent reference point, even in times of change. When values aren't clearly defined and shared, members will make assumptions and bring differing ideas of what is acceptable and valuable, then act accordingly. Values help an association create a strong sense of community, identity, and security—all of which are key to achieving increased membership, belonging, and engagement.

VALUE PROPOSITION

"What's our value proposition?" In recent years, associations have reflected on this question repeatedly because people stopped joining. Membership declined, and associations struggled to understand their purpose in this changing marketplace.

An association's ability to clearly communicate value and why someone should be a member relies on an association's ability to understand why and how personal values shifted, and why identifying and upholding core organizational values matters more than ever.

Member Values	
Then	**Now**
Hierarchy	Collaboration
Loyalty	Relationships
Community	Globalization
Advocacy	Social Awareness
Status	Inclusion
Sales	Service
Legacy	Disruption
Right Thing to Do	Return on Investment
Fellowship	Belonging

Associations struggle with their value propositions when they struggle to identify and understand the shifts that have taken place, and when they hold steadfast to their roots. Associations were founded on the premise that certain rules (bylaws) needed to be followed and traditions upheld. For centuries, everything about the association model and mindset was predictable: Products, services, events, and member benefits remained the same; traditions were passed down; and members would both literally and figuratively pay their dues, eventually gaining enough experience to sit on a committee or the board of directors. Everything ran according to expectations, process, and hierarchy.

But the world has changed. Expectations have shifted, processes have been disrupted by innovation and new technologies, and hierarchy is being replaced with new approaches to leadership and community-building.

While associations still have much to offer, the needs of the market have shifted and what associations deliver and how they deliver it must also change. What members value today isn't what they valued yesterday.

SHIFTS IN VALUE

Here's more insight on a few of the core shifts that have taken place and impacted association value propositions.

LOYALTY TO RELATIONSHIPS

Since the arrival of the home computer in 1982 and the technology boom that followed, generations of youth have been raised with access to increased information and awareness. This has spawned a greater interest in exploration—be it the exploration of different careers, cities, religions, hobbies, or lifestyles. As a result, these generations are more apt to move from one opportunity to the next, garnering them a reputation among older generations for having a lack of loyalty and "stick-to-it-iveness." This is because, for the generations born prior to 1982, loyalty was a value.

In the early part of the 20th century, society was rocked by war and recession. In the aftermath of World War I, the Great Depression, and World War II, a quest for peace and prosperity emerged. People wanted to settle in and settle down—find stable jobs, be in community with one another, raise families, and feel a sense of security, predictability, and belonging.

During this time, loyalty became a value—loyalty to country, community, job, and family. Following suit, joining an association and continuing to pay dues became renowned by society as the right thing to do. That's not the case anymore.

Young professionals aren't loyal to institutions as much as people. Effective and inspirational leaders or mentors are frequently cited as the primary reason young people will first engage with an organization. To them, loyalty is not something you do just because; it is something that is earned when meaningful relationships and great experiences are actively present.

In this time of exploration, relationships have emerged as a value.

COMMUNITY TO GLOBALIZATION

We used to be a society separated by gender, religion, ethnicity, and country. That is no longer the case. Since the mid-19th century, that which defines and separates us has become increasingly less prohibitive. Increased air travel, exporting, immigration, humanitarian and equality movements, Live Aid, and other streamed events, plus the advancements of online technology and social media, have all contributed to the redefinition of community.

I'll never forget traveling to the Netherlands and falling in love with the country's famed stroopwafel. I brought several packages home with me, anticipating that I wouldn't have the opportunity to enjoy their sweet caramel goodness until I returned. About a year later, I saw they were added to Amazon. Not long after that, my local grocery store started carrying stroopwafels. I felt equally happy, frustrated, and dismayed. I enjoyed having to travel to enjoy something new. It felt special and exclusive, but our world is getting smaller every day. Our grocery stores carry products from throughout the world, Netflix brings entertainment into our homes from various countries, and we easily connect on LinkedIn with professionals worldwide.

In the past, community was largely defined by where you lived, and membership organizations established chapters according to geography, as well. Today, our society thinks and acts globally, yet associations have lagged in transitioning to a global mindset.

Globalization is something earlier generations could only consider in abstract terms, but the generations born since 1982 have always lived it. As a result, some young people will back on the concept of associations having chapters, not seeing the need to be organized by geography and desiring to be organized by common interests instead. Others will expect streaming events, an association that is tapped into a global network and learning opportunities, and remote access to absolutely everything an association has to offer.

Every association must consider ways to be a borderless, open community. Globalization is a value, and it's here to stay.

ADVOCACY FOR SOCIAL AWARENESS

During the past decade, younger generations have grown increasingly concerned about environmental disasters, social equity, financial security, increasing college tuition, and the inaction of older generations to address these pressing issues. Today's youth and young professionals tend to be well educated, better informed, and politically conscious. They are saddled with debt, fearful of the future, and growing more frustrated by the minute.

This struggle didn't emerge overnight, and it isn't unique to the United States. Consider this global timeline over just two-years' time:

- 2009 – In Britain, students outraged by proposed tuition increases attacked the Conservative Party's headquarters in London and pummeled a limousine carrying Prince Charles and his wife, Camilla Bowles.

- 2010 – *Bloomberg Businessweek* reported on the "youth unemployment bomb," explaining the economies in Britain, Germany, Japan, Spain, China, and the U.S. couldn't generate enough jobs to absorb their young people, and "with no place to go, the largest, best-educated generation in history is making its voice heard, creating revolutions, and wreaking havoc worldwide."

- 2011 – Young people in Tunisia organized the Jasmine Revolution to bring down a dictator. Immediately following, government dictators in Egypt, Libya, and Yemen were overthrown and uprisings took place in several other countries. The old model of power based on kings and military dictators in the Middle East was blown apart by the Arab youth bulge, a generation unwilling to accept being undereducated, unemployed, and powerless.

The 2008–2018 decade was especially influential for Generation Z, the generation of youth and young adults who have come of age during an era of historical political events, including the first U.S. black president, first female presidential candidate, and arguably the most divisive political environment in history.

Add in marriage equality campaigns, anti-bullying campaigns, March for Our Lives, Me Too, Black Lives Matter, and the Global Climate Strike, and it becomes evident that in more ways than one, young Americans have been raised to be advocates.

While young people didn't learn a great deal about government and governance because of the decrease in civics curriculum in schools during the past two decades, they are socially aware and considerably more likely to link a company's commitment to a cause to their purchasing and employment decisions.

Young people don't believe government is something they can positively influence or the way to get something done. They are more likely to engage in grassroots advocacy, which is something associations need to consider. Many associations focus on advocacy in terms of lobbying for policy change and will struggle to engage young people with such a narrowly defined, at-an-arm's-length approach. These generations expect to be on the front lines. They value being empowered to use their voices and active participation for meaningful change.

FROM STATUS TO INCLUSION

A few years ago, I presented at a conference alongside a Gen Z high school student. While we waited our turn to present, a few other speakers were introduced, and the student turned to me and asked with all sincerity why the introductions for each of the speakers were so incredibly long. "I don't care about all their previous accomplishments and college degrees," he said. "What I care about is what they have to say here and now. And if I want to know more, I can just Google them."

Initially, I thought it was just a pet peeve of this one person, but I've since heard similar complaints aired by other young people.

This points to a key shift that has taken place in recent years: Leadership is not synonymous with years of experience anymore. The concepts of leadership and leadership status are shifting.

In recent years, there's been a plethora of start-ups and success stories among young entrepreneurs and change-makers who didn't have any experience. As a result, years of experience and status don't carry as much weight as they used to; rather, the next generations are counting on their leaders to deliver results. And like the student said, they have access to all the additional information they could want or need at their fingertips.

Looking through the lens of young people, it makes sense that they would question an organizational focus on experience. No longer is all the wisdom and experience contained within the eldest, predominantly white, male population. This hierarchical, homogenous model survived for centuries, but it is no longer relevant or sustainable.

The generations born since 1982 are the most racial and ethnically diverse generations in history, as well as the most tech-savvy and entrepreneurial, the most educated, and the first to have more women than men obtain postsecondary credentials. And now, there is ample evidence that companies with inclusive, diverse leadership are considerably more profitable than companies with homogenous leadership.

Leadership is not synonymous with years of experience anymore, yet many associations remain organized this way. I cringe when I hear of associations appointing board leaders based solely on seniority or title, or associations that interpret inclusion as having one young professional and one person of color on the board. In fact, I still run into boards of directors celebrating the appointment of their first female board chair or board president!

Associations need to take immediate action in this regard and reformat their bylaws and board criteria to allow for the participation of members from all ages and backgrounds. Leadership is meant to move the collective needs and interests of an organization forward. Status and experience alone can't achieve this. Inclusion is needed and valued. Inclusion is the only way forward.

FROM JOBS TO ENTREPRENEURS

It used to be that you would choose a career, get a job, and work for that industry—sometimes for the same company—until you retired. In recent years, we've seen the emergence of the Gig Economy, in which more workers detach from conventional jobs to take on contract work and other short-term gigs. Add to that the global pandemic's shift to remote work, a widespread demand for flextime, increased demands for skilled labor, and the Great Resignation, and it's obvious the world of work isn't about working nine to five anymore.

The entire workforce is moving into an entrepreneurial mindset, both figuratively and literally. This will require associations to reconsider their member benefits as well as the length of membership and volunteer terms. After all, if you juggle responsibilities or change jobs every year, you may not have the time or affinity to a profession to want to join an association.

The entrepreneurial mindset is evident in both the rising number of start-ups among young professionals and youth and the number of young people juggling multiple responsibilities or shifting between opportunities. Television shows like *Shark Tank*, *Master Chef Junior*, and *Dance Moms* all represent the shift that has taken place in society since the 2000s, moving children to a place of heightened competition, achievement, and innovation. Today, it's not uncommon for youth and young professionals alike to be juggling multiple activities, jobs, education, and be self-employed or in the process of starting up a business.

By and large, associations have been slow to recognize how this social shift influences volunteerism. Many board terms require two or three years of service minimum, with the option to renew terms two or three times. Having the same people in leadership for an extended period doesn't position associations for adaptability or allow for the infusion of new ideas from new perspectives. Moreover, lengthy terms of service aren't aligned with the flow of talent and continual transition in today's workplace.

Lengthy volunteer terms come from the stable and slow-to-change job mindset of yesteryear, yet most of the workforce now has been raised to value an entrepreneurial approach.

From Sales to Service

Associations spend a considerable amount of time and resources on membership recruitment—also known as membership sales. It stems from the Industrial Era focus on growth and productivity. Make more widgets to sell more product, to make more money. Bigger is always better. Quantity is more important than quality.

Associations hire people to sell memberships, sometimes basing a portion of their salaries on commissions. Here and now, this isn't the right approach. Retention is the best sales tool. Happy, inspired members will grow membership faster than any cold calls or digital ads. When members are miserable, the culture shifts, and people leave the association. Once that happens, it doesn't matter how many sales calls are made. The association will transition into a revolving door, with more people leaving the association than joining.

The results would be considerably more favorable if associations transitioned their sales teams into concierges. The service approach aligns with member values.

When technology became intelligent and companies like Amazon and Netflix started making recommendations based on our interests, expectations forever shifted. Today, we all expect our consumer experiences to be more intuitive and responsive to our needs. We want to be a name, not a number. We want to feel important, cared for, and appreciated.

As the member of a community—literally paying dues to belong—expectations are especially high. Members expect the association to go the extra mile to make them feel like they belong. Associations would be better off utilizing their resources to hire teams focused on creating the best membership experience possible with the people who are already invested in the community and eager to be part of it.

I felt especially important when someone from an association I belong to reached out and spent a half-hour giving me personalized guidance on how to get involved and new opportunities to leverage based on my unique career interests and needs. The time spent on this outreach call confirmed my decision to join, inspired me to get more involved, and I have since spoken highly of the organization and encouraged others to get involved.

Exceptional service deepens relationships, improves retention, and creates grassroots momentum. Members value the feeling of belonging that great service provides. When it comes to selling memberships, it really shouldn't be about selling at all.

CREATING A VALUE PROPOSITION

The shifts listed above don't just impact value, they also impact culture. Different outcomes, expectations, and behaviors emerge from different values. As a result, an association could observe shifts in how members interact with one another and utilize their memberships, as well as shifts within their workplaces and how employees interact with one another and do their jobs. Likewise, as noted in the example above, an association could influence these shifts depending on their commitment to implementing a values system.

The value proposition (also known as a value statement) should speak directly to the member's main problem, how it solves the problem, and why a membership in the association is the best solution to that problem.

The association's mission statement defines the association's purpose, whereas the value proposition acknowledges what the members need, and what the association does best to answer those needs. These are core components to consider when drafting the value proposition:

1. **Challenges:** Members join associations believing that the association can help them solve a problem. They will renew when that problem has been solved or they believe the association

is making an honest effort to solve the problem. Challenges can vary by age range and even region. Therefore, research is important. But challenges can also vary with social shifts. As this book is being written, there's an emerging focus on mental health and gender, sexual, and racial equality. These priorities emerged in the aftermath of COVID-19 and the George Floyd murder, and the rise of TikTok among other social changes.

2. **Solutions:** Members want to trust that an association can deliver on its promises. How does the association solve the challenges members have while simultaneously creating a sense of community? This is where associations need to prove their ROI.

3. **Why Membership Matters:** Members want to know there's a compelling reason to join, not just for themselves but also for others.

Writing these answers out will help the association hone its value proposition.

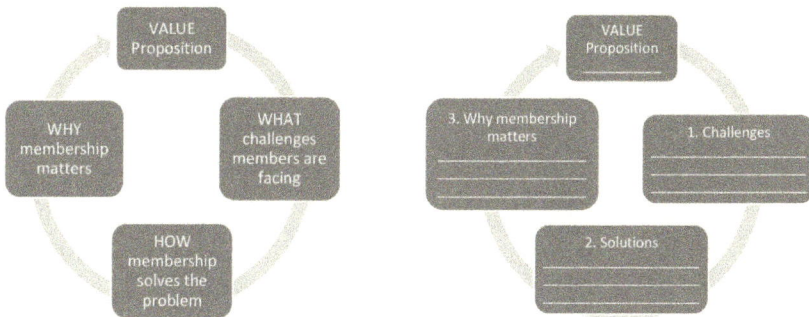

Note: It's imperative the association's value statement resonates with young people. I recommend having purposeful conversations with young members, staff, and prospective members to identify your association's value proposition from their perspectives. The association should continue the practice every two years. Values shift as social change occurs, which is happening on a continuum now.

For an association to stay ahead of the curve and respond to the changing needs of a changing audience, the association must be intentional about being in relationship with and continually talking with young people. This is key to inclusion, community-building, sustainability, and relevance.

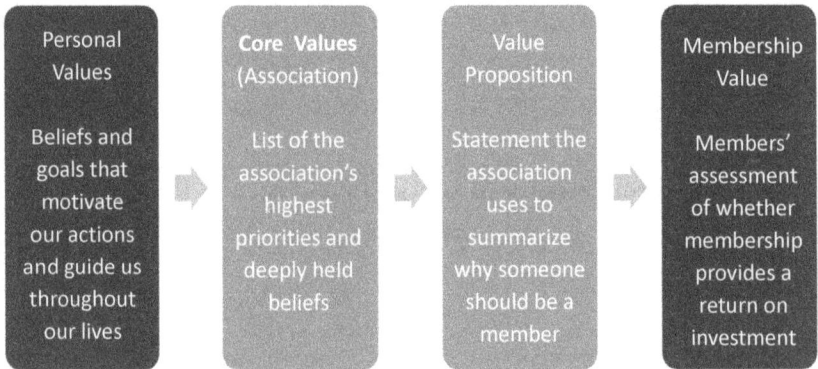

Personal Values	Core Values (Association)	Value Proposition	Membership Value
Beliefs and goals that motivate our actions and guide us throughout our lives	List of the association's highest priorities and deeply held beliefs	Statement the association uses to summarize why someone should be a member	Members' assessment of whether membership provides a return on investment

RETURN ON VALUE

There are values we hold for ourselves (personal values) and those we seek in the organizations we support (core values and value proposition). Next, we must feel there is actual value received because of deciding to join, participate, or purchase. This is where membership value and membership ROI—return on investment—come into play.

Our values influence our perception of value received from a membership. And our values are influenced by our social experiences during childhood.

Consider the following timeline:

- *Prosperity*

  World War II was over. The economy was booming, as was the population. The Baby Boomers (1946–1964) were raised to pursue the American Dream. The largest generation in history at that time would also become the wealthiest generation in history, renowned for their purchases of large homes with sprawling lawns, jewelry, recreational vehicles, and other assets. Boomers also invested in membership organizations, valuing the opportunity to support and build a community.

- *Instability*

  Gen X (1965–1981) would come of age during an era of economic instability marked by multiple mini recessions, downsizing, mergers, and acquisitions. Gen X became the first generation never to have known job security. They also became the first generation of latch-key children, experiencing mostly unsupervised and unstructured childhoods. Most Xers were raised to be self-sufficient, raised by two working parents or single parents. They didn't immediately move into membership, becoming the first generation to question membership value.

- *Recession*

  Gen Y (1982–1995), also known as Millennials, surpasses the Boomers, becoming the largest generation in history. Having come of age during the Great Recession, this generation incurred the largest credit card and college debt and faced the highest jobless rate since the Great Depression. Many Ys had to prolong milestones like marriage or living independently because of financial constraints. The concern for financial stability is evident in membership. Ys have been slow to join and quick to leave if the ROI isn't deemed high enough.

- *Pandemonium*
  Gen Z (1996–2009) came of age during the most disruptive, transformative era in history. They grew up fast in a world plagued by school shootings, climate change, protests, and the most controversial and divisive presidential races in U.S. history. During the COVID-19 pandemic, they missed major adolescent milestones and watched the economy sputter. Zs were raised to be competitive and learned early there are no guarantees. They are more likely to save money, seek positivity and stability, and pursue opportunities that can guarantee a benefit or return on investment.

When young people started questioning the value of membership a few decades back, they were labeled as slackers and the what's-in-it-for-me generation. The shift that was happening was largely ignored, dismissed, and sometimes the butt of a joke. In each instance, it was chalked up as nothing more than a youth-inspired, self-centered phase.

But it wasn't a phase, and it was deserving of considerably more attention. A new generation, one raised with different values, was viewing membership through a different lens, and they were calling for new, different, and more ROI.

As the timeline shows, membership value shifted. Not for a moment or even for a few years. Forever. This was the beginning of a new norm, one that would trickle up and influence the masses. As a result, the question of value is being raised by all age groups and why members now cite the lack of value as a reason for dropping membership. Membership value shifted, and there's no going back.

This is leading people to continuously question: Is membership a good investment?

In terms of finances, the social shifts of recent decades have resulted in more caution. We're more careful and informed consumers, and we want to ensure we will receive a return of equal or greater value on our investments. As a result, associations will experience membership decline when the cost of membership is higher than the return, and when the member benefits are easily accessed elsewhere or aren't timely, useful, or relevant. In both instances, the value of a membership is diminished.

But ROI isn't just measured in terms of financial returns. The return on investment is closely tied to personal values, connectivity, and emotion. The emotional side of membership is rarely explored or verbalized, but members are always pondering the answer to the question: Do I belong? This means membership value is determined by an association's ability to deliver a financial return on investment and fulfill a member's need to belong and be part of a community.

The chart below shows the need for ROI, both financially and emotionally. Members are likely to determine membership ROI by asking the following questions:

Membership Value Analysis	
Financial ROI *Does the value of membership exceed the cost?*	**Emotional ROI** *Do I belong?*
☐ Exclusive *Is this the exclusive, go-to resource, or can I find the same services elsewhere for less money?*	☐ Experience *Will joining bring me joy and a sense of pride?*
☐ Inclusive *Are there products and services included in the price of dues or does everything cost extra?*	☐ Inclusion *Is it easy to get involved? Are there ample ways for me to volunteer, participate, and connect to the community?*

☐ Online	☐ Outreach
Will I have on-demand, 24/7 access to member benefits?	*Does membership result in a positive shared outcome—a greater good—for community or industry?*
☐ Urgent	☐ Unequivocal
Is the association responsive to change and continuing to roll-out new services and products?	*Is the association renowned for its leadership, innovation, and ability to influence meaningful change?*

THE MEANING OF MEMBERSHIP

Imagine you're the man in the comic strip I described earlier, but instead of taking a helicopter to a mountaintop to speak to a guru, you were meeting with a group of members. You'd look at the members and ask, "What is the meaning of membership? What is our purpose of our association? What does it all mean?"

What do you think they would say?

In the comic, it's obvious the businessman is missing it. He's focused on the wrong things. His values are misaligned. The meaning of life has evaded his understanding because he's not actually thinking about life itself. He's consumed with material goods and financial success and a busyness that fails to fulfill his soul.

Apply that same theory to your association. Is it possible that delivering value to members has evaded your association's grasp because it's not focused on the members themselves? Is your association consumed with a definition of success that has little to do with serving others?

Being valuable means being both focused and decisive.

To be clear, the value proposition is for members. No one else. Some associations make the mistake of authoring value statements to appeal to entire communities or industries with little regard to members. This dilutes membership value and positions associations at a disadvantage by making their claims sound completely unrealistic or downright ineffective.

People want and need to join something important—something fraught with purpose, making a meaningful, measurable difference. That's why this value statement resonates:

"Gain visibility and build your business with our membership. Together we will improve your profits and professional future by empowering you with access to practical resources and a strong community of professional peers."

And this one does not:

"We're the voice of professionals around the world, advocating for the industry and its significant economic impact."

Your association can't be everything to everyone. You can't have it all. Going that route means eventually, the association will find itself wandering in the wilderness—or traveling to mountaintops—desperately seeking solutions, direction, and value. When all the while, the answer was right there, staring back at you.

The intent of a value proposition is to make a prominent statement about what the association stands for and delivers with excellence, and as a membership organization, shouldn't that be membership?

Membership is the mission and vision, the compass, and the call to action. Membership is, by far, your association's most valuable asset, competitive advantage, and defining trait.

Don't lose sight of what is most meaningful.

CHAPTER 4: DISCUSSION GUIDE

Reflect and respond. Write your answers in the book or download the play-book online and fill it out. Share and discuss with others in the association.

What is something society taught you to value as a child that you still value as an adult?

_____

_____

_____

_____

_____

_____

_____

_____

Member values have shifted. Is there an awareness and acceptance of change in the association? Why or why not? What actions would help the association predict change and get members feeling excited and inspired by it?

_____

_____

_____

_____

_____

_____

_____

Consider the seasons members have come of age in economically and socially: prosperity, instability, recession, and pandemonium. How is each season likely to influence that generation's values and membership decisions? What deliverables can the association provide to serve and support members raised in every season?

_____

_____

_____

_____

_____

_____

_____

_____

The association can't be everything to everyone. Who is the target market? Be as specific as possible. And within the target market, who is under-represented in membership? What steps must the association take to make room for them?

_____

_____

_____

_____

_____

_____

_____

What is the meaning of membership? What does a membership in your association offer that people won't likely experience anywhere else?

_____

_____

_____

_____

_____

_____

_____

After reading this chapter, where did you identify opportunities for improvement? What immediate changes are needed to place the association on a member-centric path?

_____

_____

_____

_____

_____

_____

_____

*Homework:
During the next 30 days, review your association's ROI—return on investment—financially and emotionally, and brainstorm ways the association could create a valuable member-centric organization.

Consider the following questions. Ask your association colleagues to do the same. Then, at the end of 30 days, set aside time as a team to share your findings with one another.

- If there were no limits to what we could do or create, what would we do to bring additional value to the membership?
- What would a best-of-the-best, most-amazing, must-have membership package include?
- What would a best-of-the-best, incredibly inspiring and fun, fear-of-missing-out membership experience include?

MAKING ROOM FOR ALL

When disengagement or decline occurs,
it's a clear indication the organization is struggling
to meet the needs of members and build a community of belonging.

Early in my career, an association took a chance on me. As the youngest person ever appointed to the board, I became part of the association's history and a symbol of its renewed focus on the future. I felt honored when I learned of my appointment, but that was nothing compared to how I felt when the board chair tasked me with spearheading a priority initiative for the association.

Imagine being told this news. You are newly appointed to the board, and you know you are making history as the youngest person ever to serve in leadership. Not only that, but you are immediately entrusted with an incredible responsibility. How does it feel?

For me, it felt humbling, terrifying, and exciting. Simultaneously given a compliment, opportunity, and responsibility, I felt proud, but also overwhelmed and eager to meet expectations. Feeling the weight of the honor, I spent hours preparing for that first board meeting, which would serve as the launch of the initiative I was tasked with overseeing.

Now imagine walking into that board room for the first time and having absolutely everything fail to meet your expectations.

Here's what I experienced.

The meeting had not yet been called to order, and the room was abuzz with conversation. It became immediately apparent there was an age difference—most people were at least 20 years older than I. Moreover, it was obvious the other board members knew one another well.

People were swapping stories about their children's marriages, downsizing, travel, health challenges, financial investments, and other personal and professional experiences I couldn't relate to as a young mother just starting out in her career. Many were sharing inside jokes and stories that can only come from years of membership, volunteering, and serving on the board together.

Immediately, I realized the connections among this group of people ran deep. Immediately, I felt like an outsider. I was thankful for the assigned seat at the boardroom table because no one reached out to welcome me or initiate conversation. My presence was largely ignored.

The meeting progressed, and I was anxiously awaiting the time set aside for my presentation. When the moment finally arrived, the board chair announced the initiative I was overseeing was being tabled until the next board meeting. I felt incredibly disappointed, but I didn't let anyone know. I just smiled, nodded my head, and told myself the delay would give me extra time to prepare.

When the next board meeting rolled around a couple of months later, I was especially excited to present. My name was again listed on the agenda. Time was set aside for the board to hear my recommendations. Surely, this time I would be given the opportunity to speak! Yet again, I was told there were other more pressing issues, and I would need to wait until the next board meeting.

This same scenario continued to play out meeting after meeting, and I began to wonder: Was I the token young person on the board?

Whether it was intentional or not, I was treated differently than other board members. I didn't have any support, and I was stripped of any voice and responsibility. It didn't take long for me to start feeling like I was invited to sit on the board to represent an idea, not a reality.

This isn't just my story; this is a relatable experience for many people. I've volunteered and worked for, consulted with, and researched associations for two decades. My experiences and data collection indicate an unfortunate and often unspoken truth: Despite being organized as communities of belonging, associations often fall short on the community-building and belonging spectrums.

How did this happen? For starters, when membership decline became the trend, it wasn't taken all that seriously. Still today, disengagement is shrugged off as something temporary, a quick fix, or something entirely outside of the organization's control. One unfortunate stock response I've heard repeatedly is, "Oh well. What are you going to do? People just aren't joiners anymore."

This simply isn't true.

Perhaps the ways in which people engage have changed, but last I checked, belonging is a core human need. We all need to feel connected to communities. It's in our nature to be joiners. The "people just aren't joiners" excuse has been the go-to for decades, giving associations blatant permission to ignore, exclude, and overlook the needs and interests of entire populations of people.

When disengagement and decline occur, it's a clear indication the organization is struggling to meet the needs of members and build a community of belonging.

Unfortunately, associations failed to heed the call for change. The fact is, it was easier to exclude anyone new than it was to include them.

After all, the larger community represented more challenge and change. Demographics shifted. Technology advanced. Pressure increased. It wasn't membership as usual anymore, so it became easier to maintain the status quo and simply do more of the same. As a result, associations became hyper-focused on serving the needs of their most invested, long-term members and stopped responding to the needs and interests of new members. Therefore, belonging took a backseat.

Belonging ensures everyone's insights, commentary, and perspectives aren't just heard, but encouraged. Simply including people is not enough. As with the board experience I shared at the beginning of this chapter, it's not enough to invite people to sit in the room and then refuse to give these individuals or entire groups of people any influence, power, or voice. Associations must strive to create a sense of belonging for all people. Then, and only then, will membership organizations succeed at creating resilient, relevant, growing membership communities.

But there's work to be done. As it is, associations are utilizing membership models and practices that prevent them from creating cultures of belonging. Sometimes, it's not noticeable because these practices are so ingrained that they've become second nature.

In my work with associations, I've identified two significant hurdles that pop up and create detours, sidetracking any efforts to build member-centric communities. My viewpoint might not be popular or even welcomed, but I believe governance and culture are largely to blame.

In this chapter, I will describe the challenges within existing governance and culture models and share solutions for transitioning to models that are more inclusive and member centric.

Governance	→	Revamp the governance structure to allow for an accurate representation of the membership community, the active participation of new volunteers, as well as association-wide succession planning, relationship-building, and diversity of thought.

Culture	➡	Shift the culture to make a significant difference in how effective an association is at recruiting and retaining members and generating revenue.

Let's start at the top.

Outdated
Bylaws and
Models of
Governance

GOVERNANCE

As far back as the 1600s, associations were founded on the premise that certain rules needed to be followed and traditions upheld. The social contract between associations and members has remained the same for centuries: The association provides products, services, events, and member benefits for a fee, and the members pay their dues, then participate in and support the association, eventually gaining enough experience to sit on a committee or the board of directors.

In recent decades, this social contract has changed.

The shift began with the Civil Rights and Women's Rights movements of the 1960s and 1970s; both fought for equality, inclusion, and representation. At the time, women and minorities didn't have a voice or a seat at most tables—nearly all decision-making roles and circles of influence were filled by Caucasian men. Other demographics had limited access to career, education, and income opportunities. As a result, leadership roles in nearly every industry were limited to one demographic, and associations were no exception.

Civil Rights was the first significant social change and technology was the second.

In the early 1980s, the home computer hit shelves and technology transitioned society in more ways than one. Prior to this point, organizations were governed by a hierarchical, military-style of leadership culture prevalent in, and mastered during, the previous several centuries. Tradition, stability, and loyalty were valued. But after technology went mainstream, an entirely new set of values and way of work emerged. In this new era, innovation, flexibility, and speed are valued.

Technology changed the way we live, work, and do business. But technology also radically changed the position of young people in society.

Anyone born since 1982 has been raised with access to technology, giving them considerably more access to information and education and global networks, plus platforms to openly share their views. They have acquired entirely new skillsets while pioneering a world fueled by innovation and technology. As a result of the tech boom, these generations had access to new career paths and unprecedented opportunities to develop new products, businesses, and personal brands.

Why is this important information to consider in your work as a membership organization? Because, for the first time in history, every generation has something to learn and something to teach. For the first time in history, every generation has a voice. The barriers to entry and opportunity have disappeared, which means the way associations are governing and community-building must change.

Civil Rights and technology forever changed the concepts of membership and belonging. In the past, associations could be exclusive and hierarchical and steeped in tradition. These were acceptable practices back then. But today, it's increasingly evident these approaches leave little room for innovation or change—much less belonging.

Today's membership organizations need to be fueled by innovation and inclusion. Society started moving in this direction in the 1960s with the emergence of the Civil Rights and Women's Rights Movements. Yet, I still hear members and association staff describe their organizations as slow to change, out of date, aging out, or a good ol' boys club.

Half a century after key social transitions occurred, associations remain rooted in the past, uncertain which tactics to deploy to modernize and create something of meaning and relevance to members.

Here's what needs to change.

"BECAUSE WE'VE ALWAYS DONE IT THIS WAY"

Just seven words have the power to stop an organization's community-building efforts dead in its tracks. Whether it's a tradition that has been passed down for generations or written in the bylaws, just because it's always been done this way isn't a valid reason to continue doing it.

Bylaws and the failure of associations to review and update them regularly hampers progress. More importantly, outdated bylaws and traditions may contribute to practices steeped in discrimination and exclusion.

For example, I recently presented at an association event and was surprised to see the use of a dais—a stage with a podium—placed in the middle of long tables where the association's officers sat facing the audience. Even during interactive portions of the meeting, the board remained seated and did not participate. It was as if there was an invisible wall separating the board from the large group of assembled members.

When I asked some of the board members why they remained seated and physically separated from the members, they each shrugged their shoulders and said, "Because we've always done it this way." After the question was raised, they realized they didn't have another, better answer. Suddenly, they were looking at each other and making statements like, "I never thought to question this. Is it still relevant? Why do we do this, anyway?"

Sometimes, traditions are so ingrained that association leaders never question their modern-day relevance. In this situation, the question to consider is, How does an association foster community-building when the leadership literally distances themselves from everyone else in the group? The answer is obvious. It doesn't.

Another example of tradition derailing community-building efforts happened recently, when I asked an audience of volunteer leaders about what's holding progress back within the association. One of the chapter leaders immediately yelled out an answer: "Because it takes 15 years to be considered for board leadership!" This was followed by clapping and comments from other chapter leaders criticizing the fact that board opportunities have largely been reserved for men. Why? Here again, the answer was simply, "Because we've always done it this way."

The "because we've always done it this way" excuse leads to very unfortunate outcomes for associations, including conflict, burnout, disengagement, and decline. Regrettably, the statement is sometimes used as a valid reason to exclude people.

I'm writing this book in the year 2023, and just this year, I've heard some commentary from association leaders that suggests these leaders aren't being mindful of inclusion, community-building, or belonging. Comments like:

- We're not doing anything virtual. If you can't get to the meeting, you can't participate.
- People who work remotely, part-time, or are on maternity leave are excluded from board leadership.
- We take care of U.S.-based chapters first. Chapters in other countries must fend for themselves.
- There are no board terms. You can stay in leadership as long as you want.
- Volunteer leaders are required to be at least 40 years old.

- Board members are expected to give significant financial contributions. Young people aren't invited to lead because of this.

In each of these instances, the excuses to keep these practices alive were the same—either "because it's in the bylaws" or "because we've always done it this way."

Neither is acceptable.

Bylaws are a legal document to dictate how the organization must be governed, and they are often misunderstood and misrepresented. One critical element often erroneously omitted in the bylaws is the provision for amending the bylaws in the future.

In the past, bylaws largely remained the same for decades at a time. There wasn't a need to change them because society largely stayed the same. That's not the reality of today, and it is the responsibility of the association and its board to keep the association's bylaws relevant and reflective of the era in which we currently live. Times and circumstances change, and your association's governing document should reflect those changes.

Bylaws weren't intended to be the equivalent of the Ten Commandments, carved in stone for all eternity. If the bylaws need to be amended to reflect current realities, do it! Don't wait. I've seen far too many associations forced into making decisions that negatively impacted the association, driving members away, simply because the bylaws were outdated, and the association had no other choice but to abide by them.

FAILURE TO MODERNIZE

The excuse "because we've always done it this way" inevitably holds associations back from modernizing. I was shocked when an association leader I met at a conference shared with incredible pride that her association had just made a bylaw change for the first time in over 150 years!

What motivated the change? Language in the bylaws that referred to notifying members by *telegram*.

This person was so incredibly excited about the bylaws update, and all I could think was, *What took so long?* And, *Wow. She has no idea how difficult it's going to be for the association to survive under that laggard mindset.*

When the pandemic hit, the world relied on technology to communicate, and some associations who previously thought themselves tech-savvy realized they weren't tech-savvy at all. In some cases, systems, equipment, and knowledge needed a major reboot. Individuals challenged by the new reality felt especially out of sorts and often lamented aloud, "I can't wait for things to go back to normal."

But isn't the use of technology normal in our society?

As mentioned earlier, the home computer arrived in 1982, and society has been gravitating towards more virtual and remote realities ever since. Entire generations have been raised never knowing life without technology. Yet, in recent years, I have worked with associations who are still communicating by fax machine, haven't updated their websites or contact databases in many years, and don't use social media. And many quickly set aside anything virtual or remote to return to normal after the worst of the pandemic subsided.

By today's standards, outdated technology, or the non-existent or minimized use of technology, is a means of member exclusion.

There are members who don't have the financial means or the employer support to take time off work to travel to events. There are members who travel often and live in remote areas or other countries. Consider the many reasons members may, at any point in their lives, be unable to readily access the association—such as caretaking, parental leave, health issues, job changes, work demands, or pursuing a degree. Discontinuing or limiting virtual connectivity shuts the door on the engagement of these potential members.

Furthermore, anyone born since 1982 expects your association to be accessible and on demand, technologically speaking. Technology is an established social norm, and it continues to advance. It's imperative that your association prioritizes the use of technology, realizing it is a direct pathway to inclusion, accessibility, community-building, globalization, and growth opportunities.

At least annually, all board members should re-familiarize themselves with the bylaws and ask whether they reflect the current state of the world. Whenever "because we've always done it this way" pops up in conversation, that's an opportunity to ask yourself why the association is still doing it and if it carries the same weight, relevance, and importance today.

It's also imperative to consider whether the bylaw or tradition is interfering with community-building. Simply accepting the way things have always been done is negligent and irresponsible.

An association's purpose is to represent and rally on behalf of a membership community. That's something that will never change, but the bylaws and traditions will need to change to support the purpose. No tradition or bylaw should derail an association's attempts to build a fair, respectful, equitable, and inclusive community.

THE SOLUTION: A MEMBER-CENTRIC GOVERNANCE REVAMP

In 2018, I pitched a book idea to a publisher about the need to restructure boards of directors. I joked we could title the book *The Big Board Blow-Up*. I laughed, but the people on the receiving end of the pitch did not. I backtracked, assuring them it was just a joke.

Turns out it wasn't about the joke.

My pitch was promptly shut down as something bordering on the impossible. The publishing team was adamant. Boards and bylaws were sacred. Never changing. Principles of purpose and tradition. People would get upset. The book would become controversial. It wouldn't sell. Writing a book suggesting boards be revamped was, they told me in no uncertain terms, a terrible idea.

Much has happened since then, like the George Floyd incident and a global pandemic. The gaps and inadequacies in those "sacred" and supposedly "never-changing" models are especially obvious now.

It's an abomination to avoid the subject and keep doing things the same simply because it may stir up some controversy and make people feel uncomfortable. The fact of the matter is that most associations are relying on governance models that are no longer sustainable or relevant in today's world. This is contributing to disengagement and decline.

Change is desperately needed. Now.

Below is a list of characteristics I believe every board must have to effectively govern associations today.

DIVERSITY BY DESIGN

When everyone on the board is close in age and has similar professional experiences and backgrounds, their perspectives, worldviews, and ideas tend to also be similar. They are viewing the association and the membership experience via the same lens. Homogeneous thinking emerges, and the boardroom becomes an echo chamber, literally producing similar ideas and perspectives repeatedly. This is when the word stuck pops into play as the association increasingly struggles to spur innovation and progress.

In addition, these organizations struggle with inclusion as leaders make decisions in the absence of diversity. When leadership isn't reflective of the diverse community it represents, gaps are inevitable because the process of governance either turns into guesswork or a self-serving opportunity. Any way you approach it, omitting diverse representation in governance is a recipe for disaster.

A different approach is needed.

Change is happening faster than ever. Associations need to be nimble and responsive to the disruption and the changing needs of members. The way an association is governed greatly influences the membership experience, and considering recent changes in the world, governance needs to be redesigned to make room for more diversity, including diversity of thought.

This means being intentional about bringing members of varying ages, skillsets, experiences, and perspectives to the decision-making table. By doing this, the association's leadership is not only reflective of its membership community, but the association is considerably more likely to innovate, anticipate trends, team-build, and create a membership experience that is relevant and responsive to member needs.

Cognitive diversity is a proven method. A study by Nielsen discovered teams comprised of a variety of skillsets, backgrounds, and roles perform 58 percent better than homogenous teams or individuals.

As the saying goes, "Teamwork makes the dream work," and there's a need for associations to be intentional about appointing cognitively diverse teams. Community-building requires connection, collaboration, and representation, and it must start at the top.

BUILD A LEADERSHIP PIPELINE

One of our daughters has nearly waist-length hair, so clogged bathtub drains are a common occurrence in our household. There's nothing worse. No one wants to get in there and pull that tangled mess up and out of the drain. But until the clog is cleared, there's nothing happening. Absolutely nothing. It stops the flow of water dead in its tracks.

The analogy is gross, but it's an accurate metaphor for what's happening in leadership. When the phrase "There is no leadership pipeline" comes up, it means there isn't any planning or process in place to allow people to step into leadership. The drain is clogged.

As a result, a core group of people repeatedly sits at the helm, becoming an immovable object.

The problem is multi-faceted. As was evident in the story I shared at the beginning of this chapter, close-knit relationships form, and a club mentality emerges among the long-standing group of leaders, excluding other people from wanting or knowing how to get involved.

The leaders who are repeatedly called upon develop an unhealthy relationship with the association, and this typically leads to one of three outcomes:

- *The commitment to service and representation dissipates into ownership.*
  When this happens, leaders feel essential to the organization's survival. Irreplaceable. I've seen some leaders struggle to manage the emotion, becoming ego-centric or power-hungry, micro-managing others or pushing their weight around and making demands.

- *The commitment to service and representation leads to burnout.*
  When the same leaders are stepping up, eventually there's a breakdown in passion or production. Burnout can be physical, but more often, it's emotional. Too many meetings. Too many responsibilities. Too much pressure to lead the association to success.

  Burnout shows up as a change in behavior. The once in-spired, talkative leader sits quietly on the sidelines. Excuses are made and participation wanes. Once burnout occurs, it's difficult to reignite a leader's enthusiasm. Moreover, it becomes increasingly difficult to convince other leaders to step up and serve once they've observed the burnout experience.

- *The commitment to service and representation is overshadowed by disengagement.*

  The opposite of what happens when leaders become overly invested, these leaders stop paying attention altogether. Auto-pilot kicks in, and a careless, apathetic attitude emerges. Burnout isn't an option because these leaders have quietly quit and faded into the background. They stop reviewing the board materials and stream a football game or respond to emails during meetings. Sometimes, they don't show up for board meetings, and when they do, they are most excited about the social time following the meeting.

For far too long, these outcomes have just been accepted. There is no way to get around it because current processes allow the leadership pipeline to remain clogged. I think this is unacceptable, and I believe there is a solution.

Volunteer leadership can and should be managed given the changing demands of the marketplace. Managing leadership participation to inspire participation and increase engagement and build a leadership pipeline starts with revamping your association's bylaws and governance model to be inclusive and representative of the entire membership community.

Some guidelines to incorporate into the revamp:

- *One role at a time*

  In some cases, associations permit members to serve in more than one leadership role at one time. This squelches an opportunity for other people to serve and creates a scenario where too few people have too much power and ownership in the association.

- *Inclusion is included*

  The association needs to be intentional in its efforts to engage new leaders and make room for them. My favorite best practice comes from an association that revamped bylaws to require at least 30 percent of every decision-making entity in the association to be comprised of members within their first five years of professional experience. This commitment to cognitive diversity and community-building breathed new life into a stagnant, struggling association. It immediately and significantly changed the entire association's outlook and trajectory, driving relationship-building, increased member engagement, and growth.

- *Avoid appointments*

  When leaders are tasked with appointing other leaders, this creates a barrier to entry for new people and creates a clique mentality within the association. In a situation like this, it's all about who you know, which prohibits participation and community-building. There's also a heightened risk of appointing colleagues, friends, or leaders who don't want to lead but say yes for the wrong reasons, such as the opportunity to spend more time with a friend or to avoid letting down someone they know or respect.

- *Limit the terms*

  A few decades back, long-arch thinking was prevalent. It wasn't uncommon for people to join a company and work there until they retired. Likewise, it wasn't uncommon to join a board of directors and serve for 10 years or longer. Stability and predictability were valued. But today, our world is moving to a very different rhythm. Today, disruption is prevalent, and innovation is required. Long-arch thinking is a thing of the past, yet board governance remains firmly planted in that realm. A re-vamp is required to allow for the continual influx of new ideas and new people and allow the circle of engagement to expand. Ideally, associations would stagger terms so there is never a large group of people leaving their leadership posts at one time, and terms would be shortened to a maximum of three years.

- *Allow for pop-ins*
  As the demands on people's time have expanded, time has become a precious commodity. Research indicates volunteerism is shifting. While most members want to volunteer, many are limited by personal or professional commitments and want ready access to opportunities to volunteer as their time and schedules permit. Give your all or give nothing isn't a sustainable or inclusive governance model. Episodic and short-term volunteering are becoming the norm, which is why the association should offer more than one way to volunteer.

- *Size it right*
  Leadership is supposed to add value to an association, not slow it down or kill momentum. If the board isn't adding value, then either you have the wrong people at the table or you have too many people at the table. (In some cases, maybe it's both.) In the past, success was measured by quantity. Today, it's measured by quality. It's not about the size of the board; it's about whether the board can provide the guidance your association needs to engage members and succeed in today's marketplace. Quality over quantity.

- *Consider the cost*
  Association leadership often comes with a hefty price tag. Volunteer leaders in board or committee roles are often expected

to participate in a myriad of meetings, conferences, programs, and retreats. These commitments often require travel or time spent away from work. In addition, some associations request that volunteer leaders give money to the organization's foundation or fundraising initiatives. The costs associated with volunteering can prohibit the participation of some members, especially young professionals. Carefully consider whether there are barriers to entry to volunteer and implement ways to offset the expense, such as offering discounts for leaders or complimentary event passes. In addition, consider the ROI for the time members take away from their jobs or families to volunteer. Identify the real, bottom-line return on investment the association offers volunteer leaders. Having this information prepared will be key to engaging new volunteers.

Governance—leadership—influences culture. Who is leading, how, and why influence what the members believe and how the members behave.

Consider the example of Google.

In 1996, two students at Stanford University conducted a research project that would eventually grow into a business earning $50 billion in revenues and attracting one million job applicants each year.

From its inception, Google became renowned for having a workplace culture that was truly revolutionary. The free cafes, funky offices, and games were the most renowned, but it wasn't the perks that drove the company's success.

Rather, Google was built on the knowledge that people want meaningful work, knowledge of what's happening in their environment, and the opportunity to shape that environment. Google understood what motivated employees and created a company based on those motivations. Google excelled at creating an exceptionally engaging company culture that resulted in exceptionally high employee engagement.

Consider the culture in your association. Does the association know what motivates members? Is it focused on meeting member needs? Does it strive to wow members and exceed their expectations?

Your gut reaction may be to say yes to all these questions, but the data proves otherwise. If associations were closely aligned with member interests and needs, engagement wouldn't be waning. The trajectory of widespread membership decline indicates most associations are making incomplete, flawed assumptions about what their members want, and struggling to create the experiences they want.

As with governance, a revamp is needed. Associations need a culture shift.

Toxic and
Exclusive
Organizational
Cultures

CULTURE

The membership experience, also known as culture, makes a significant difference in how effective an association is at recruiting and retaining members and generating revenue.

Culture is evident in every interaction your association has with its members. It's how members feel when they talk to staff on the phone, visit the association's website, attend an event, read a publication, post to the social media channels, join a committee, or meet the board of directors.

The feelings members experience whenever they interact with the association—good, bad, or indifferent—are powerful influences. The association could do amazing projects or provide unique services, but if members don't feel good about the membership experience, they won't engage.

Culture has always been important, but right now, it's crucial, largely because of technology. Members expect their experiences with the association to be intuitive, on demand, customized, and fast. Young members are wired for more choices, information, and access. Membership experiences need to transition because member expectations have transitioned. There is little to no tolerance today for experiences that are lagging, negative, irrelevant, stressful, or disorganized.

Culture matters in membership engagement. Here's what needs to change.

TOXIC BEHAVIOR

In some membership organizations, bad behavior is permitted. A few examples I've observed first-hand:

- Name-calling, shouting matches, and emotional outbursts
- Demanding room upgrades at conferences
- Drunk and disorderly conduct
- Posting discriminatory remarks or political commentary on the association's social media channels
- Watching football games during board meetings
- Using the association's credit card to purchase massages and rounds of golf

These behaviors negatively influence and define the organization's brand, culture, profitability, and growth potential. It's difficult to community-build when the leaders create or permit chaotic, unhealthy environments, and neglect their responsibilities and commitment to serve the members to the best of their abilities.

Sometimes, association leaders think the toxic elements of the organization's culture remain well-hidden from the members. They don't. Despite the best efforts, people can sense when a culture isn't stable.

Early in my career, I worked for an association struggling to maintain a positive culture. Within a three-year timeframe, three different executive directors led the organization, and 19 people on the staff transitioned in and out of the organization. Chaos ensued and shifted the culture. Senior leadership kept telling the staff to remain calm, act professionally, and go above and beyond to serve the members. One leader repeatedly told us, "The members only know what they see. They don't know what they don't know."

But it quickly became obvious we weren't hiding anything. The jig was up. Membership declined. Revenue declined. Sponsors left. Board members disengaged, and staff turnover resumed. That experience ended up being a defining moment in my career, and I eventually left to start a consulting company working with membership associations.

Culture is powerful. Within a short period, I watched an association's fate swing radically from success to struggling, largely because of a lack of leadership that spurred a shift in culture. What's unfortunate is the association never fully recovered from that era of instability. Positive momentum? Yes. Recovery? No. The outlook and potential of that organization was drastically changed.

BAD REPUTATION

Whether it stems from leadership or membership, toxic behavior is ruinous to an association's efforts to community-build and grow membership.

Consider the story of the client who contacted us with concerns about membership decline. The association was puzzled by what was causing the sudden slide, so for the first time in more than a decade, a survey was distributed to members. The staff was shocked to discover the level of dissatisfaction directly tied to an organizational culture that was running rampant in the association.

The survey indicated members didn't trust the association to deliver what they were promising. This distrust resulted from negligence and the mismanagement of funds under a former executive's leadership many years before. The leader had long since left, and the situation was resolved, but members were still feeling the aftershocks of this experience. As a result, members were seeking reassurance and more information and outreach from the association. The lack of communication contributed to their feelings of distrust, fueling negativity and disengagement, and even feelings of inequality and a lack of value without the staff and board realizing it.

This is a reminder that culture is heavily influenced by leadership, but there are instances when culture becomes rooted in, and harvested by, the community itself. Like a virus, it spreads, spawning rumors, criticism, and beliefs, sometimes without the association being aware of it. Therefore, associations need to continually survey members and assess the health of their organizations.

It's kind of embarrassing to admit, but I've been the member of an association for 10 years now and have never participated beyond watching a couple webinars. Some people would describe me as a checkbook member—someone who pays dues but never participates. Why do I do this? Because the word on the street is the association's membership isn't especially friendly.

I've met current and former members alike, and they all say the same thing. I have yet to hear the in-person experience described positively, so I've never felt compelled to show up. I continue to pay dues because I believe in the organization's mission and find the publications and resources useful. But that's the extent of the relationship.

Sometimes, I wonder if the association even knows they have a bad reputation. I wonder how much this culture problem is costing them in terms of membership and revenues. Moreover, I often wonder how it's possible that after a decade of membership, not one person has reached out to invite me to attend something or get more involved. The lack of outreach confirms to me the rumors are true, and it's not an especially friendly or member-centric community.

SCARCITY THINKING

No matter how you slice it, membership comes down to emotion. Participation, engagement, and belonging are all outcomes of how people feel when they are interacting with your association. There's a small group of people in every association who feel genuinely inspired, passionate, connected, and included. The question is, is this enough? Should associations be content to have a core group of committed members and not concern themselves with expanding the circle of engagement?

In my work with associations, I've observed there is a scarcity mindset. Scarcity thinking is the belief there isn't enough to go around—not enough money, time, or recognition. In the association realm, I see the mindset emerge when there's a lack of focus.

It is a well-known and accepted practice for association staff to work extra hours under stressful conditions, often because the association mismanages resources and time. Between government relations, business and industry relations, event planning, community and public relations, and chapter and volunteer relations, association staff can find themselves running on a continual hamster wheel, attending numerous meetings and events, and working on several projects and deadlines at one time. Where are member relations in all of this? It's in the mix but rarely the priority.

Not surprisingly, scarcity thinking pops into play because staff is on the verge of burnout, and there is a fear that there is already too much work to do and not enough people to do it. By thinking this way, associations contract the circle of engagement, limiting their potential to grow, and sometimes excluding people in the process.

The scarcity mindset reveals itself in comments like these:

- If we engage young members, we risk alienating our older members.

- Members in the rural areas are feeling overlooked, but that's just the way it goes. More members live in the city, so that's where we need to focus our energies.
- Our chapters are complaining we don't provide enough resources to help them serve members at the local level, but that's their job, not ours.

Scarcity thinking in associations comes from a place of overwhelm and distraction. In each of these examples, the member experience and service to members is compromised. The focus is on the wrong priorities when an opportunity to improve or expand the membership community is put on the backburner or dismissed.

US VS. THEM

Steve Jobs, co-founder of Apple and Pixar Animation Studios, believed there were two types of organizations: those that foster a grassroots intelligence network, and those that create playpens and separate people into groups.

According to Jobs, an organization with a grassroots network encourages people to collaborate, share ideas and problem-solve together, and learn from and challenge one another. In contrast, the organizations with the playpen approach tend to focus on productivity and profits. There isn't much cross-pollination, so these teams rarely look at things from a different perspective, which limits the potential of the entire organization.

When you think about it, there are many ways associations separate people into playpens. Here are just a few examples I've observed first-hand:

- *Board operates independently of the staff*

Yes, it does happen. In fact, I worked for an association that requested the staff not interact with the board. In these cases, only the association president has a line of communication with board members, and board and staff remain mostly estranged, working independently of one another.

- *Student or young professional groups are treated as a separate entity*
  Some associations make the decision to launch a peer network for young members. While there are benefits to doing this, the situation backfires when associations fail to also establish meaningful relationships with the young professionals. I know of associations that experienced significant membership losses when their young professional groups split off and launched their own entities. Other associations struggle to transition young professional members out of the peer network and into regular membership, observing drop-offs shortly thereafter.

- *Executives only*
  Do any of these statements sound familiar?

  o Only people with 15 years of experience can serve on the board.
  o Only the senior staff are permitted to speak at team meetings.
  o Only board members and senior staff can sit in the chairs at the front of the room.
  o Only executives attend the conference because they're concerned another company might meet and steal their young talent.

There are many traditions and practices that exclusively celebrate hierarchy, experience, and longevity. Too much emphasis on hierarchy and exclusivity counteracts community-building efforts and prohibits the participation of new people with new ideas. Furthermore, wisdom and ideas are no longer synonymous with executive status. Access to information and education and the advancement of technology have resulted in the expansion of knowledge and skills for people of all ages.

The more playpens and separation that exist in an association, the more likely the association is grappling with membership turnover, negative cultures, and a lack of innovation. A culture of competitiveness emerges because members are essentially ranked and prioritized and given access and opportunity according to their experience levels and career stages. As a result, there are entire groups of people who feel like they don't belong, and this creates conflict, disengagement, and decline. The us-versus-them approach is fueled by hierarchy, an outdated leadership model detrimental to community-building efforts.

THE SOLUTION: SHIFT TO A MEMBER-CENTRIC CULTURE

In this era of disruption, recession, pandemic, climate change, terrorism, and school shootings, what people want most is a place of security, acceptance, predictability, and happiness. More and more, your members will seek to avoid experiences that are negative, stressful, disorganized, or draining of their time and energy.

There's been such a resistance to negativity and toxic cultures that the concept of cancel culture emerged. The practice has been referred to as a mob mentality encouraging lawlessness, censorship, and the erasing of history. It's also been referred to as a long overdue way of holding people accountable for propagating racist and sexist ideas, toxic behaviors, and making unethical, immoral decisions without any concern for others. Cancel culture is accommodated by considerable controversy and debate; both are indicative of a bigger trend.

People hate feeling irrelevant. Disregarded. Overlooked. I have heard this lament repeatedly in my intergenerational work. Conflict emerges when people feel like no one is listening to them. Feeling ignored drives people to disengage, quit, protest, and cancel.

Conflict is the outcome of not listening to and respecting one another's points of view. Until we can improve on that skill alone, social unrest, employee turnover, and membership disengagement and decline will continue.

Below is a list of traits I believe every association must have to create a positive culture and community of belonging.

- *Inspire excellence*

  Everyone who interacts with the members needs to understand the association is in the service business, and the culture they create for your members plays a critical role in the association's ability to succeed. This is an awesome responsibility. It never ceases to amaze me how often volunteers and members alike give associations low marks on our surveys for service and responsiveness to their interests and needs. Mediocrity in membership shouldn't be the accepted norm. I recommend the association provides training for staff, chapter, and volunteer leaders to ensure they understand how to successfully build community with members of all ages and create an inclusive, welcoming membership experience. Mediocrity is simply not good enough.

- *Focus on abundance*

  Have you ever sat in a board or staff meeting and someone says, "We don't want membership to continue to decline" or, "We won't be able to change"? If your team is consciously and unconsciously focusing on decline, you'll probably just get more decline. The scarcity mindset sets the association on a destructive path. Instead, focus on what you want to change. Start by gathering the team and writing down what won'ts, don'ts, and can'ts are holding the association back. Next, write down what the team will and can achieve. Flip the script to focus on abundance.

- *Learn and teach*
  Social shifts in parenting changed how children were raised. In the mid-1990s, children started influencing the majority of household purchasing decisions. As a result, today's young professionals are accustomed to being asked their opinions and having a close relationship with leaders and mentors. They hold leaders accountable and seek to have a relationship with them. In addition, technology brought an influx of information, access to education, and the development of new skillsets to young people. For the first time in history, every generation has something to learn and something to teach. Research indicates the associations with leaders who intentionally set aside time to meet with, learn from, and build relationships with young people are considerably more successful at community-building and engaging members. The set-aside can take many forms—mentoring programs, think tanks, advisory boards, or coffee chats. The point is to take the time.

- *Win*
  The cycle of engagement changed in the 1990s. My research indicates Baby Boomers and Gen Xers have a roll-up-your-sleeves approach to membership. They are more patient when challenges arise and are willing to take the time to tinker and fix whatever ails the organization. In contrast, Millennials and Gen Zs expect the association to run smoothly. A positive environment matters to them, as does an organization that gets

meaningful results and makes things happen. This raises the question of whether associations are tracking their wins and gaining their members' trust that they can deliver on their promises. There will always be challenges that pop up, but associations can also do a better job of showcasing their success and commitment to members. I recommend creating a dashboard to succinctly communicate key achievements and track measurements of success. The dashboard would be updated monthly at a minimum, appearing on the association website and newsletter.

- *Recognize and repeat*
  Sending a pin to members on their membership anniversary isn't enough. Associations should aspire to create a culture of recognition and celebration. Doing so will result in higher levels of engagement and feelings of pride. Start by developing a campaign to continually spotlight members of all ages, career stages, job types, and regions who represent the values and ideals of the association. Launch a Membership Awards program and include categories to recognize those who are currently being overlooked and under-represented. Organize pop-in visits at member companies. There are countless ways to recognize members in meaningful ways, and culture will inevitably shift when membership becomes something to celebrate.

- *Fun-raise*
  Early in my career, I worked for a leader who launched a fun-raising committee. The goal was simple: Plan fun activities for the staff to do together. When we're children, a lot of our education is focused on play, creativity, and using our imaginations. As we age, less time is spent tapping into this side of our brains. We can become so ingrained in policies and procedures

that we forget to have fun. I encourage our association clients to bring elements of surprise and fun to all they do, even board meetings. One of my favorite examples of this happening was a client who had staff unexpectedly crash the board meeting, dancing into the room with cupcakes and balloons and the song *Celebration* blaring. The staff all wore the same t-shirts and briefly took over the presentation to showcase recent association achievements. Everyone loved it. Videos and photos of the occasion show the impact it made on people, who were laughing and cheering. Fun-raising works.

- *Ask*

  The only way to know if your association is meeting members' expectations and providing value is to ask. We're living in an era of continual change. To stay ahead of the curve is to stay in close contact with members. Polls or short surveys disseminated throughout the year is a good practice. At minimum, I recommend surveying members on an annual basis. Don't try to guess what members want. Ask.

MAKING ROOM FOR ALL

Governance and culture. It all comes down to these two organizational traits. How your association leads and how your association makes people feel is the difference between success and failure in today's market.

When this happens...		What you're really saying to the membership community is:
"Because we've always done it this way"	→	Change isn't an option. New ideas aren't welcome here.

Failure to Modernize	→	We don't prioritize being relevant or keeping members informed. We're comfortable falling behind.
Toxic Behavior	→	It's acceptable to be malicious, dishonest, careless, and irresponsible. We don't value integrity or respect one another.
Bad Reputation	→	We don't know what our members think, need, say, or do. We don't really care.
Scarcity Thinking	→	Only certain people, projects, and initiatives are deserving. Our limited resources won't allow for inclusion or expansion.
Us vs. Them	→	Stay in your lane. Stick to the status quo. The members with the most experience are the most important.

Do a gut check after reviewing this chart. How does it feel to read these words and phrases?

When our firm does research with members and prospective members, sentiments like these often pop up, and the phrasing strikes a chord when it is presented to the association's staff and board. Often, the team is shocked, saying things like, "We had no idea our members felt that way! We didn't realize we were making people feel isolated, frustrated, or like they didn't belong. We want people to think positively about our association. We don't want to be considered outdated, irrelevant, or exclusive. We realize now that a change in approach is urgently needed."

Membership growth is impossible until the existing membership feels confident a membership in the association makes a meaningful difference, their needs and interests are being addressed, and they feel proud to be a member and connected to the organization.

Back to my youngest-person-in-the-room board experience. After a year of being backburnered, I resigned. I left feeling disappointed. Foolish. Betrayed. I never did get the opportunity to present my ideas or lead the initiative as promised.

Thinking back on it now, it's clear the association wasn't ready for me. How could they be? They were wielding an outdated governance model that had failed to modernize and lacked a leadership pipeline. They didn't understand their culture wasn't inclusive. They thought it was enough to just give me a seat at the table.

There's a lot of talk about concepts like inclusion and belonging, but research shows that despite their best efforts, associations have, in large part, struggled to create communities of inclusion and belonging in recent decades.

As the saying goes, you can't make an omelet without breaking a few eggs. It's time for associations to break tradition to create something of relevance. It may feel uncomfortable, but in the long run, the revamp of governance and culture practices is the only solution. Consider this: If associations can't lead effectively, and they can't succeed at delivering great experiences, what are the chances of their survival?

Time is running out. It's time to stop talking about change and make it happen. Associations must be restructured as communities of inclusion and belonging.

CHAPTER 5: DISCUSSION GUIDE

Reflect and respond. Write your answers in the book or download the play-book online and fill it out. Share and discuss with others in the association.

Think of a time when you felt like you didn't belong. What did that experience feel like? What could others have done differently to welcome or include you?

_____

_____

_____

_____

_____

_____

_____

_____

Which of the following roadblocks are preventing the association from reaching its full potential? Check all that apply.

- ☐ "Because we've always done it this way" = Resistance to change.
- ☐ Failure to modernize = Decreased relevance, acceptance with falling behind.
- ☐ Toxic behavior = Malicious, dishonest, careless, or irresponsible actions occur often.
- ☐ Bad reputation = Lack of communication leads to the formation of rumors, myths, and negativity.
- ☐ Scarcity thinking = The belief of limited resources prevents progress or improvement.
- ☐ Us vs. them = Lack of inclusion leads to competition and conflict.

What are three steps the association could immediately take to remove these roadblocks?

1.

_____

_____

2.

_____

_____

3.

_____

_____

Is the association ready for new people with new ideas? Why or why not? What actions would help the association adopt a people-first, future-focused approach to membership?

_____

_____

_____

_____

_____

_____

_____

_____

_____

After reading this chapter, where did you identify opportunities for improvement? What immediate changes are needed to place the association on a member-centric path?

_____

_____

_____

_____

_____

_____

_____

*Homework:

During the next 30 days, review the roadblocks to engagement—governance and culture. Consider the following objectives chart and discussion questions. Ask your association colleagues to do the same. At the end of 30 days, set aside time as a team to share your findings with one another.

| Governance | ➡ | Revamp the governance structure to allow for an accurate representation of the membership community, the active participation of new volunteers, as well as association-wide succession planning, relationship-building, and diversity of thought. |
| Culture | ➡ | Shift the culture to make a significant difference in how effective an association is at recruiting and retaining members and generating revenue. |

- What specifically needs to change to establish a board that reflects our diverse membership community?
- What specifically needs to change to create a culture of belonging?
- What can we commit to doing in the next 30 days to start the process of transitioning our governance and culture to something more member-centric?

A Strategy for the Future of Membership

A member-centric organization has a membership strategy, not a business strategy.

When I ask association leaders about their membership strategies, I usually receive one of three responses:

- "What membership strategy?"
- "We outsource that."
- "We just throw spaghetti at the wall and see what sticks."

In other words, when it comes to membership strategy, associations tend to fall into one of these buckets:

- Those who don't have a membership strategy
- Those who think membership strategy is a job to be delegated
- Those who do it themselves, knowing very little about membership strategy and hoping something will eventually work

Membership strategy. How much do we *really* know about it? At the beginning of the book, I posed this question. With no defined requirements, career paths, educational tracks, or training programs dedicated to membership, there's much that isn't known about membership strategy.

Resembling something more like a game of hot potato, approaches to strategy have been tossed around somewhat haphazardly in hopes of finding a solution that works—delegate, outsource, just go with your gut, or borrow ideas from nonprofit and business leaders.

But membership is an entity unto its own. It's not like any other business model. Borrowing concepts from other models or experts in those areas, leaving it up to chance, or throwing in the towel altogether isn't going to get associations where they need to go.

There is a better way.

After considerable research and testing, I've identified the five fundamental elements of a membership strategy proven to yield results.

Member-Centric Membership Strategy

Future-Focus
Members First
Co-Create
Diversified
Research

Let's delve into each pillar in greater detail.

MEMBERS FIRST

Pause for a moment to consider all the work that's being done in the association. Picture it in your mind. Think about the many projects, meetings, events, and outreach occurring on a daily, weekly, and annual basis. Think about your responsibilities and the many projects, meetings, events, and outreach you plan, develop, create, and do on the association's behalf.

Now ask yourself: How much of this work is solely focused on and dedicated exclusively to the members?

Take all the industry leaders, public officials, sponsors, prospective members, non-members, and anyone else who isn't paying dues to your organization completely out of the equation. How many programs are planned for members only? How many meetings are held with members only? How much outreach?

Before you read any further, write down the number you are thinking of in the space provided here. Use a number between 0 percent and 100 percent. On average, what percentage of the association's work is dedicated exclusively to members?

_____%

Early in my career, I worked for a membership association. If I was asked to sum up the experience in one word, it would either be busy or chaotic. Everything felt urgent and everyone was busy, so very, very busy. The back-to-back meetings, incessant emails, multiple deadlines, and constant pressure to produce, plan, and get things done put everyone on edge. It was the office equivalent of an emergency room.

And yet, membership was declining, staff turnover was increasing, and board members were absent. Despite all the running around and efforts to switch things up, the metaphorical ship was sinking. Fast.

The reason why is very clear to me now. It's because membership wasn't the priority.

A considerable amount of time was being spent doing tasks that didn't directly impact the members. Make no mistake about it, much work was being done to benefit the lives of many people. But the members were just one of many audiences in the mix. There wasn't a clear focus on, or benefit to, the members themselves.

Rather than being first on the list, the people who most invested in and needed the association the most were often being placed last.

Beware of the busy virus. Too much busy-ness is an indication the organization's health has been compromised.

Consider how people talk about the work they do in the association. Whether they are staff or volunteers, the language that's used is a good indication of how people are feeling. Is the team more likely to describe their work in the association as busy or inspiring?

Regrettably, busy is a word I often hear association executives and volunteers use to describe their state of being, and every time, I cringe. I'm immediately transported back to that previous work experience, and all the stress and scurrying around that only served to push the association away from its purpose. Putting members first means members are the priority. All the time. No matter what. It means the focus on the members is evident throughout the entire organization, even in how the work is done and what work is being done.

Every membership organization should aspire to get to 80. At least 80 percent of the association's work should be exclusively focused on the members. Think back to the number you wrote down. If the number is low, it's an indication the association has lost focus and is stunting its growth.

In Chapter 4, I shared the M1 commitment at Nexstar Network and their "membership is everything" approach to building community. This is a model that has yielded year-over-year success because the association is solely focused on the membership community and member experience.

A member-centric organization has a membership strategy, not a business strategy. That means rethinking the path to growth. A business strategy touts revenue growth through concepts like expansion into new markets and revenue streams. In associations, this strategy backfires. In associations, the bottom line relies on how well the association invests in the membership—not just part of it, but all of it.

Creating a member-centric association begins with how the association works. These are the defining characteristics of a member-centric organization:

- The association is committed to equipping members with the tools, education, and resources they need to advance their careers and unleash their potential.
- There's a laser-focus on membership and the development of membership metrics. The association discusses member retention and ROI as much as revenue.
- Members are continually invited to share their ideas and feedback and their views are included in the membership strategy.
- There's an effort to incorporate young members into every layer of the organization to allow for inter-generational community-building, succession planning, innovation, and to ensure the association is serving the needs and interests of all members.
- The association fosters a culture where all members are empowered to make decisions, serve others, and voice their opinions and are continually appreciated, recognized, and valued.

To succeed, associations must recommit their organizations' focus to the members. Imagine if your association was dedicating at least 80 percent of its time to members and the positive momentum that would inevitably follow.

Imagine what would happen if your entire team woke up tomorrow and proudly stated:

"We're starting fresh! We're in the membership business now. We're going to be the best we possibly can be for our members. We're going to pull in the best experts, build the best curriculum, and find the best tools to ensure their success. We're going to invest in new technology and build streamlined systems to better serve members. We're going to go above and beyond to show our appreciation to them. Everything we create, plan, or do will be designed by and for the members."

Transitioning an association closer to the 80 percent mark has the potential to increase value, drive growth, and generate revenues. If at least 80 percent of the association's time was focused on members, then engagement, participation, and belonging would skyrocket, as would word of mouth and the number of prospective members.

Building a member-centric organization is not the same as building a business or nonprofit. Remember:

- It's not about being accessible to as many people as possible.
  It is about forging close relationships with the paying customers—the members.

- It's not about being mediocre at many things for many audiences.
  It is about being the best at serving the members.

- It's not about being busy or on the verge of burnout.
  It is about being intentional and inspired.

- It's not about building business.
  It is about creating a community of belonging.

- It's not community first.
  It is members first.

DIVERSIFIED

Diversified is a term commonly used in the realm of investing. It's the practice of spreading your investments around so exposure to any one type of asset is limited. The same methodology is used in member-centric strategies with a few alterations.

The asset in any membership organization is membership, and when it's done well, associations can build an engaged, growing community.

First, it's important to note the membership strategy I'm going to share will feel counter-intuitive to the strategies used in other realms. Most of us are familiar with business and investment strategies, which rely on a transaction-based approach to financial growth, but this will not work with membership. Frankly, this approach is kryptonite for any association seeking membership growth.

For example, business strategies urge companies to go big and scale by continually seeking ways to bring in more customers. Most businesses are built on transactional relationships. It's rare for customers to engage with the same business every month over the course of many years. As a result, businesses must continually fill their pipeline of customers.

But membership is a relationship. It's not a product or a transaction. It's permanent, and it's something to which people feel committed and attached.

Think of membership like a tattoo on the heart; the decision to join an association is choosing to have membership be part of their daily lives. They are choosing to make an emotional and financial investment and foster a relationship with the association, its mission, and community.

Investment strategies rely on a similar approach to business simply because financial markets fluctuate and money floats in and out of our lives. To grow your nest egg, investment firms will encourage you to "move your money around" and "play the market" rather than just invest in one asset for the next several years. Acquiring new and different investments increases your chances of financial gain. Here again, the strategy is not permanent. It's transactional and temporary. No tattoos here.

Associations need to rely on a relationship-based strategy instead.

For membership organizations, the potential to scale stems from continuing to re-invest in its asset (membership) and continually diversifying the deliverables to increase the membership's value and meet the changing needs of the membership market.

According to my research, when social change occurs, it influences value shifts, which ultimately influences what members need, want, and expect from their membership experiences. To stay relevant and valuable, associations need to understand their community's needs and what behaviors and deliverables will drive future success.

Business and investment strategies lead associations to think it's wise to add more revenue streams, like conferences or events, providing open access to both members and the public. The equation aligns perfectly with business and investment strategies:

Accessible to Everyone = Event Revenue + Awareness + Potential to Attract New Members

It is mistakenly believed that this approach will yield results. If it did, membership decline wouldn't be trending for more than 60 percent of associations for more than a decade.

When it comes to diversification in membership associations, the strategy to offer more or larger non-member deliverables is an ineffective way to provide membership value. When this happens, the core asset membership organizations have—membership—becomes endangered.

Disengagement isn't the result of an association being invisible, unknown, or needing to be accessible to prospective members. Disengagement happens when the value of membership declines. When members aren't the priority and a membership fails to provide something valuable, relevant, and meaningful to its audience, members disengage.

Diversification in membership associations is the exercise of adding as much value to the membership as possible and giving members a clear advantage over anyone who isn't a member.

Examples of diversification in a membership strategy include the following:

- Reviewing the list of member benefits on a regular basis to measure return on impact to the members
- Adding new must-have members-only products and services to the membership offer
- Surveying members on a regular basis to determine their challenges and needs, then developing products and services to help them address or resolve those challenges
- Delivering value to members of all ages and career stages to ensure everyone has equal access to services that benefit them personally and professionally.

RESEARCH

What's holding your organization back from reaching its full potential?

Would other members answer the same question differently? Do you know for a fact how they would respond?

I started my career as a journalist. Whether covering police reports, corporate financials, or lawsuits, you quickly learn the importance of fact-finding. When lives and reputations are at stake, you must know, behind any shadow of a doubt, the information you are conveying is correct.

Perhaps it's my background in media coming into play, but I am often surprised by the number of association leaders running their organizations blindfolded, comfortable navigating the unknown and making assumptions or guesses on the next best steps. Their decisions aren't data driven or research based, so it shouldn't come as a surprise when their organizations struggle to engage members.

A few years ago, a client told me he was lying awake at night worrying about what the survey data would reveal. "What if it's bad news? I really think I'd prefer not to know," he said.

Can you imagine having a close friend who never wanted to hear your ideas, opinions, or get your feedback on anything? The person never asked how you were doing or what you were thinking or feeling or questions about your favorite anything. Every time, the conversation was only about your friend. It was never about you. Would you still consider that person a friend?

Likely not.

Would that person know you very well?

No.

And what if this person bought you a gift, and it was something you didn't need, want, or even like?

This is what associations do when they fail to engage their members in conversation or ask for their feedback. Associations become the annoying friend whom you try to distance yourself from and eventually drop altogether.

Don't think of research-gathering as evasive. Research is an opportunity to get to know your members better. Plus, knowledge is power. It's always better to have the opportunity to fix whatever ails the organization rather than ignore it and just hope everything will work out for the best.

Research in a member-centric organization looks like this:

- Short surveys administered often to capture quick insights and stay informed of how current events or changes are impacting members

- Dialoging with members throughout the year in a variety of ways, like think tanks, coffee chats, roundtables, town halls, panel discussions, social media polls, and live chats
- Setting aside time at least once a year to research and analyze trends or discuss shifts in values and behavior that may impact the industry, community, or membership within the next 5 years

CO-CREATE

Here's something you probably haven't thought about before: Membership is a science. Association teams need to think like scientists.

Science is the process of gathering evidence, learning through observation and experimentation. It's also understanding how our emotions impact our cognitive processes, such as how we learn, make decisions, communicate, reason, and make sense of the world.

This means, as I just covered in the last point, that research is required for associations to clearly understand the needs, interests, and values of members and stay informed about how each is changing over time. In addition, associations need to continually strive to establish an emotional connection with members. Brain and social development have evolved in recent decades, which means members of younger ages are having a different emotional response to your association and membership than previous generations. The only way to fulfill the emotional part of the membership-is-science equation is to co-create the membership experience.

When community-building is a staff, board, or leadership initiative, it will be considerably less effective than a membership initiative. It must be a team approach.

It's scientific. At the most basic level, people want to feel a sense of belonging. Consider all the positive emotions gained by bringing people together:

- Co-creating aids leaders greatly in easing their fears, making it possible to adapt and accomplish change.
- When members feel invited and empowered to help, they feel a sense of purpose, which leads to higher levels of trust and membership engagement.
- When people of different ages, skillsets, experiences, and backgrounds work in collaboration with one another, productivity and innovation skyrocket, and people feel enthused about the work they are doing.
- When members see how their contributions benefit the association, it gives them a sense of pride.
- Co-creating has been proven to increase energy, creativity, and productivity, which generally leads to less-stressed, happier, and more engaged members and staff.

Collaboration is the word most often used to describe the teamwork and alignment being described here, but I'm choosing to use the word co-create because it's more descriptive.

I believe associations need to work on their community-building efforts. For so long, hierarchical models have overshadowed associations, pushing them away from any community construct. The word co-creating reminds us we're starting at the beginning. This is a new opportunity and a new beginning. We're engaging members throughout the process, co-creating the vision and path forward to build the community from the ground up.

In member-centric strategies, this is how co-creating shows up:

- All members have a voice and are encouraged to introduce new ideas.
- Leaders actively seek the feedback of mentors, think tanks, advisory boards, young professionals, and students.

- Every decision-making entity, including the board of directors, is cognitively diverse, reflecting the diverse ages and backgrounds represented throughout the membership community.
- Stakeholders are empowered; members of all ages and backgrounds are passionate about the association and will support the association on a change-making journey.
- Members and volunteer leaders collectively determine the course of action to best serve and engage the membership community.
- Members and volunteer leaders collectively implement the membership strategy.

FUTURE-FOCUS

Is your association a generation ahead or a generation behind?

In 2015, for the first time in 34 years, the world's population started trending younger. Today, more than half our world is under the age of 30, and the workforce majority is under the age of 39. Yet associations aren't following suit. The average age of membership has continued to increase, as has the amount of decline among young members.

Furthermore, childhood and adolescence are influential years in terms of brain and values development, and the youth of today are experiencing more change during their youth than any other generation. Paying close attention to what impacts the youth in our society, and how they respond, are windows into the future. These impacts are evident in the following trends, which are just a few of many that associations should consider when contemplating their futures:

Creative Uprising
Youth have taken to the streets to protest and rally for change, and they create videos and other ways to hold companies and leaders accountable. This activism is an indication of how the

membership audience is shifting. Young people will expect your association to walk the walk, not just talk the talk. They will expect the association to be part of an ongoing conversation, leading and influencing positive change. They will also demand a voice and a seat at the table.

Connectivity

Associations have unprecedented opportunities to reach more people than ever before. How can you connect—really connect—with your audience from here on out? Humanize your brand. Go to your audience and engage them in dialogue. Ask them what they need. Listen, and create something new and relevant and meaningful. The more you can get members involved in your brand, the better.

Education and Training

Gen Z consumes more content than any other generation, turning to numerous sources for learning and inspiration, including YouTube, *Shark Tank*, TED Talks, and TikTok. Due to workforce turnover, skills gaps, and worker shortages, young people will be on a fast-track to leadership and expected to learn new skills quickly. This provides opportunities for associations interested in workforce development, skills training, and certification programs.

To expand on that last point, workforce development is a pressing need globally. This is not a new issue. Workforce development started to become a concern in the late 1960s, when demographers realized that the generation of children being born—Generation X—was a much smaller population by comparison to the Baby Boomer generation. There were concerns then about talent development, mostly due to the difference in population sizes.

Today, we're not only concerned about population, but we're also concerned about skills and education gaps, the diversification of jobs, the evolution of technology, retirement waves, and the Great Resignation.

What worked in the past isn't working anymore.

To build a growing economy for generations to come, every organization has a role to play, but few are as well-suited to solve the workforce crisis as membership associations. This requires associations to be future focused and to work in close alignment with young professionals and students, as well as industry and education leaders.

The current state of associations, with the majority reporting flat or declining membership, indicates an urgent need to create environments inclusive of, and in collaboration with, young people. If associations focused on achieving this, an immediate upswing would occur.

In member-centric strategies, these are some examples of what being future focused looks like:

- Membership is offered to high school students and college students.
- The association provides education, job training, scholarships, and certifications.
- Every decision-making entity, including the board of directors, is at least 30 percent comprised of young professionals currently in their first five years of a career.
- Various workforce development initiatives exist within the association, such as leadership training, career fairs, job shadowing, certification programs, and job site tours.
- The association provides training programs for member companies struggling to manage and develop young talent.
- Young professionals and students are invited to present on panels.
- The association's vision is revisited annually, and time is set aside to plan for the association's future and the strategy to get there.

THE FUTURE OF MEMBERSHIP

What would you create if you were starting the association over? Imagine you woke up and—poof!—the association wasn't there anymore. You are given the opportunity to rebuild it from scratch. What would you create?

It's an important question to consider because that's what you're being asked to do.

Membership organizations are in crisis. Decline has been steadily worsening since the 1990s, with the majority now reporting flat or declining membership. There's no way to sugarcoat it. Membership organizations are struggling to recruit and retain members and compete amid rapid change. But every crisis presents an opportunity.

During a crisis, traditional approaches and paradigms are challenged. Motivations change. Discoveries are made. New collaborations and ideas emerge. Crisis offers the opportunity to create something different and equally, if not more, valuable. Crisis is an opportunity to rewrite the future.

Consider this book your wake-up call, the moment to shift focus and to stop doing whatever it is that wastes your association's resources and draws attention away from the membership community. Cut the clutter, kill the sacred cows, stop the mediocrity, and narrow the focus.

It's really very simple. Members leave when there isn't a place for them to belong. So, make room. Take the time. Invest in the relationships. Create a place where members of all ages and backgrounds can belong. Put the members first, and your association *will* reverse the decline and observe exponential growth.

The time is now. Don't wait. Shift your association's focus on to the members.

Do it now, before it's too late.

CHAPTER 6: DISCUSSION GUIDE

Reflect and respond. Write your answers in the book or download the play-book online and fill it out. Share and discuss with others in the association.

On average, what percentage of the association's work is dedicated exclusively to members?

_____%

What actions could be taken immediately to create an internal shift in focus and workload?

_____

_____

_____

_____

_____

_____

Is the association a generation ahead or a generation behind? What is needed to be even more future focused?

_____

_____

_____

_____

_____

_____

Membership as a science requires the association to know as much as possible about the members and be in relationship with them. What changes are needed in the association to make both of those happen?

_____

_____

_____

_____

_____

_____

Do you feel like the association is in crisis? Why or why not?

_____

_____

_____

_____

_____

After reading this chapter, where did you identify opportunities for improvement? In your opinion, what immediate changes are needed to place the association on a member-centric path?

_____

_____

_____

_____

_____

*Homework:

During the next 30 days, review the questions below. Consider the following objectives chart and discussion questions. Ask your association colleagues to do the same. At the end of 30 days, set aside time as a team to share your findings with one another.

- What would you create if you were starting the association over? Imagine you woke up, and poof, the association wasn't there anymore. You are given the opportunity to rebuild it from scratch. What would you create?
- What's your vision for the association? Has it changed since reading this book? In the next 12 months, what significant accomplishment or change would you like to see the association achieve to place it on the path of being member centric?